AC Pearls
Writing A Legacy

Copyright © 2023 by Alexis N. Clark

www.acsvisions.com

Dedicated to Hubby,
Machiah, Autumn, Alexis,
Apphia, and Avigail

"Shout out to the team, nothing without the whole grind!"

COMPASS
Inventor Services

AC Pearls

Writing a Legacy

Written By
Alexis N. Clark

Contents

Chapter 1. **The Purpose of AC Pearls**
1

Chapter 2. **Relationships & Partnerships**
13

Chapter 3. **Lions & Lionesses**
36

Chapter 4. **Self-Criticism & Destructive Thinking**
59

Chapter 5. **Transition & Transform**
88

Chapter 6. **Insecurities & Projecting**
117

Chapter 7. **Self-Love & Boundaries**
142

Chapter 8. **Conclusion**
170

The Purpose of AC Pearls

When I was in my early 20s, I enjoyed reading non-fiction books. I loved finding men and women who would challenge and inspire me through the pages of memoirs, self-help, and motivational publications. I have always had an insatiable appetite for learning and broadening my perspective to help cultivate my ways of thinking. My goal has always been to become a better version of myself.

For over a decade, I built a library that fed my intellectual and spiritual hunger. It helped me understand the challenges I was going through and prepared me for those seasons of life I knew would be difficult. As a teenager, I read self-empowering books from writers who taught me the principles of success in business, cultivating emotional intelligence, understanding human behavior, coping with difficult bosses, and how to manage conflict. As a single mother, I gravitated towards books that would help me to be intentional as a parent, develop the skills needed to break generational curses and prepare me for marriage. While I had a head start on what to expect once I did get married, I had a lot to learn. During the early years of my marriage, I sought out books to help foster deeper connections with my spouse, manage arguments better, and understand how to be a better companion. I especially enjoyed books that uplifted and motivated women, encouraged wives, and equipped mothers.

After having five children of my own, I desperately needed to hear from women who had gone through the mental health challenges I was wrestling with as a stay-at-home mother. I also needed to hear from men who dealt with similar struggles in their relationships, as it offered perspective on what Hubby was navigating through and how I could better support. Sadly, many books I came across were too watered down for my taste. Too generic and safe. When dealing with a problematic adolescent man-child and four daughters, all under six, I needed an honest and raw perspective. When Hubby and I bumped heads, I needed wise words from an older woman to help me determine whether I was experiencing the typical marital growing pains or losing my mind. In the darkest moments of my life, when I lost my way, I needed to hear from a woman who had been through similar seasons of depression and anxiety. I have always had a healthy appetite for reading books that captivated my attention, shocked my senses, challenged my reality, and spoke truth to my heart. Very few books have been able to leave a lasting impression on the analytical mind I possess. The books that made the greatest impact on my life would eventually be referred to as "my pearls." I collected these pearls of wisdom from authors who were not afraid to be vulnerable and honest. They gave it to me straight and were unapologetically transparent and authentic. These were authors who shared their success stories along with their failures. Their stories compelled me to search my heart and examine my spirit. They moved me to make purposeful adjustments to how I carried myself as a young woman and take accountability for my choices in life. Pearls are precious gifts that are created and shaped by natural pressure over time. We harvest and arrange pearls to wear as jewelry and accent our clothing. Pearls are presented as gifts to the people we treasure most. Authors like Priscilla Shirer and Chrystal Evans Hurst gave me precious pearls throughout my twenties. Men like Tony Evans, the Benham Brothers, and Daniel Fusco dismantled my broken views of men and helped me to see the complementary design God intended for men and women in a marriage. By the grace of God, these gifted authors have been my mentors throughout my adult life and the early years of my marriage. Their books left a lasting impression on my life. I can look back and pinpoint the specific moments I read their pearls of wisdom and utterly had my mind blown. I carefully highlighted, underlined, and reread paragraphs to glean transformative truths that made my heart smile and encouraged me. Through each season of my life, those pearls helped shape the woman I am today.

After almost a decade of marriage and five children, finding a book that could speak to my current season of life and encourage me just as powerfully was a challenge. I'd exhausted my inspirational reserve and was hungry for a fresh perspective. It was a season of potty training, homeschooling, marital woes, depression, a hormonal teenager, and an identity crisis. I needed tangible help navigating career choices, mental health challenges, family drama, and rediscovering myself apart from being a wife and mommy. Sadly, I have yet to come across a book that could speak to me as powerfully as they once did. In hindsight, the lack of external inspiration forced me to contemplate my own convictions about marriage and family life. Subsequently, I created my own pearls from life experiences. My views on womanhood, love, relationships, parenting, and much more are precious pearls that I have developed over time. They are foundational to the woman I am today, how I function in my marriage, and how I raise my children. In early 2019, I began to lose sight of my purpose and passions in life. In 2020, life served me a full plate of grief and marital hiccups with a side of pain and mental health scares. I took the time to audio record my pain, what was going through my head, and random epiphanies. Over time, those audio recordings helped me develop my 'AC pearls of wisdom.' Pearls that I hoped to share with my children one day.

I had a twin brother. His death in 2020 shook my soul. It also birthed a sense of urgency within me. Death has always served as a sobering reminder of the transience of life. It reminds us that we do not have as much time as we tell ourselves. No one knows the day or the hour. As a result, time is the most valuable commodity in this life. If we don't know how much time we have, shouldn't we use it as wisely and deliberately as possible? After two years of talking into an audio recording app, I finally started to write the book I was looking for. Writing this book has not only provided me with tremendous healing and relief, but it has also helped me rediscover myself. My thoughts on self-worth, creating healthy boundaries, learning how to use my talents effectively, and child-rearing have become new passions. The purpose of *AC Pearls* is not to air out my dirty laundry. It's not meant for readers to get a kick out of the messiness of my life and marriage. The intentionality behind *AC Pearls* is to inspire, encourage, and give a fresh perspective on how we view ourselves, function in relationships, and live out our purpose. Rarely do people bare their hearts and sins to their friends, family, or children to gain a more productive perspective on how to live life well and make better, more informed decisions.

Many parents and caretakers aren't equipped to teach their children how to navigate life's challenges in a healthy, positive, and powerful way. We typically paint the best version of ourselves because that is what we want them to see, yet we still expect them to be their best authentic selves. How does that work exactly? When we don't model transparency and authenticity in day-to-day relationships, children become confused adults who struggle with fundamental human interactions. When they come to mommy, daddy, grandparents, uncle, or auntie for guidance, we display a shallow and superficial version of ourselves. We give thoughtless and theoretical advice that we muster up in the moment. You know, the kind of advice that sounds good, but you have never personally tested or witnessed its transformative truth for yourself. It sounds good because a well-respected psychologist on relationships spoke about it on a podcast, right? It worked out well for your favorite reality TV couple, right? Most people can look back and remember those seasons in life that challenged, shaped, and molded their identities. Those moments contribute to the trajectory of our lives, marriage, and family for the better or worse. We can pinpoint the moments where we took a wrong turn, had a lapse in judgment, and failed epically. I can remember having to clean up pieces of broken relationships, eat humble pie, or sleep where I pooped. Many of us are living with brokenness and have yet to muster up the energy to begin the work required for healing and restoration. I remember moments when I spoke cruelly to a coworker, hurt someone I loved, or made a friend feel like crap over a moral lapse in judgment. Those memories and how foolish I was in them still haunt me. I may never have reconciled those mistakes, but I have learned to move forward and find peace.

We desperately want our children to have healthy marriages, families, and home lives, yet we are not willing to be radical in how we teach, guide, and mentor them toward that goal. Instead of being vulnerable and giving our children the best and worst of ourselves, we often hide behind our insecurities and throw scraps of advice at our children from behind an empty shell of a person. Real and positive change begins once we emerge from behind the fake persona that took years to create. It starts by practicing being open and honest with yourself rather than defaulting and hiding behind the facade of a persona you've grown into. Admit when you have no freaking clue. Don't be afraid to tell those stories about how you messed up. We abandon our children to fend for themselves because we never learned better. Not that we didn't know better. We never learned better. Most parents wouldn't dare tell their children that they had an extramarital affair, an abortion, a secret love child, wrestle with mental health challenges, deep-seated insecurities, or debilitating anxiety. Parents usually don't tell their children how the hero they look up to took decades to mature into. My now 18- 18-year-old son was fortunate enough to witness his teenage mother evolve into the woman my four daughters have known all their lives. However pleasant or ugly the process, I want all my children to see how mommy and daddy deal with conflict, get on each other's everlasting nerves, love, and work to keep our family together and thriving.

Since I was a teenager, I have always had what many of my friends and family viewed as radical beliefs about love, marriage, and family life. All that I've learned of love in the Bible and how God designed us to be in relationship with one another only fueled my seemingly radical ideas about how the family was designed to function. After almost ten years of marriage, five children, and nearly four decades of living, I want to give my children something that parents are rarely willing and able to offer: Pearls. The kind of pearls that will serve as guides for them along life's rugged roads. Perspective and insight are what transform young and impressionable minds. There are three things I have tested and found to be critically important in my life. They are pillars that served me well; from a young girl to a single mother, throughout adulthood, as a wife, mother of five, and home educator. Being authentic, living courageously, and having a vision for yourself and your family are the pillars that freed me to live life differently than what was modeled for me or considered the social norm. Upholding these pillars has been a lonely resolve at times, but when I talk to my now-adult son, I believe it to be God's grace that helped me to be consistent in my resolve.

Some may read this book and question the value of baring it all. However, most people know the percentage of broken marriages in the United States today and how young people treat relationships as transitory and fluid experiences. It's terrifying and appalling. It is also beyond time for a fresh perspective on the matter. Something radically different from what social media and reality television have to offer. *AC Pearls* is meant to encourage, empower, and motivate readers toward positive change. My pearls may also help inspire men and women to rediscover the best versions of themselves, strengthen marriages, and encourage parents to find more meaningful approaches to connect with their children. These are all the things I desperately wanted to read about as a teenager, a single mother, a woman in the workforce, a newlywed, and a stay-at-home mother. I pray the thoughts and discoveries written in this book will stir up a sense of urgency in your heart to make better, more intentional, positive, and sustainable life changes. I am hopeful that this book will resonate with people of various demographics, spark more honest conversations, and be the catalyst that leads to beautiful transformations. Whatever season of life you find yourself in, *AC Pearls* will refresh and inspire you.

Relationships & Partnerships

I gave birth to my son, Machiah, at 19. Two months shy of my 20th birthday. It had barely been a year since I graduated from the Naval Recruiting Training Command in Great Lakes, Illinois, in the fall of 2002. Machiah's father and I met when I was in high school. He lived in Chicago, Illinois. I lived in Asheville, North Carolina. We maintained a long-distance relationship for almost a year before I joined the Navy. I distinctly remember telling him of my intentions to enlist. It never crossed my mind that he would have a problem with my decision. He told me our relationship would be over if I joined the Navy. He wanted me to move to Chicago with him, get married, and immediately start a family. I was more curious about his objections than offended. It was one of the first times in my life that I questioned why anyone would want to hinder my ambition to do something with my life. I loved the thought of starting a family, but I was in no rush. It was definitely something that I wanted, just not at 18.

Marriage and children were not a priority for me at that time. I wanted to see the world, get an education, and start a career. On July 9, 2002, I enlisted in the United States Navy and was on the next bus to Naval Recruit Training Command. When I told my boyfriend I enlisted and was shipping out, he was true to his word and ghosted me. It hurt, of course, but the excitement of a future in the Navy overwhelmed whatever heartache I felt toward him. I was beyond ready to get on that bus to start my new career and leave everything behind.

I was surprised to receive a letter from him while in boot camp. I didn't expect to hear from him ever again. Looking back, I wonder how he even knew where to send the letter. Shockingly, his attitude about me joining the Navy did a 180° turn. He expressed his happiness about my career choice and was excited to see me in uniform. He also promised to be the loudest person in the crowd at my graduation ceremony. I was happy that he came around and was hopeful we could still be a family one day. The day I graduated from boot camp, three people were in attendance to support me: my parents and my baby sister. About one month after graduation, we reconnected, and I agreed to meet up with him. He apologized for missing the graduation and wanted to start over. I was so focused on my new career that, again, being heartbroken was not on my radar. Sure, I was disappointed, but it didn't matter. The excitement of starting trade school was everything to me at the time. On my days off from school, I took the train from Great Lakes to the South Side of Chicago to visit him. A few months into trade school, I became pregnant. I remember the nurse telling me that I did not have the flu. I was having a baby. I also remember telling her, *"No no, no no no."* As if she couldn't possibly be correct in her diagnosis. When I told Machiah's father the news, initially, he was overjoyed and could not wait to tell our families. I was pleasantly surprised and unprepared for his excitement. In hindsight, I wasn't sure how he would react to the news of my pregnancy. The question of whether or not it would be a problem for him was higher on the list than excitement.

The news of my pregnancy left me in a state of shock. I didn't have the headspace to think too deeply about how he would respond. Needless to say, the excitement didn't last long. Two weeks later, reality set in. He called me out of the blue and told me he wasn't ready to have a baby. In my mind, I thought, okay, thanks for letting me know. I told him I was keeping the baby. After an earful of him expressing his manic concern over not being ready for fatherhood, he hung up and wasn't heard from for another 18 months. The man dropped off the map. He ghosted me so badly that I questioned if I'd imagined him some days. However, the life growing inside me reminded me he did exist and that I wasn't crazy. He just didn't want to participate. I was young, unwed, fatherless, pregnant, and scared. The only positive thing to come out of that terrifying situation was my unwavering desire to be a good mommy. Once the shock of my pregnancy settled in, I was fully committed to my child's well-being. Although the relationship with my son's father was non-existent, I had a new relationship with the child growing inside me. That season taught me a lot about relationships and what the word truly meant. I had never taken the time to critically think about my views on relationships or what I wanted from one. Sure, I thought about what kind of man I wanted, how many children we would have one day, and daydreamed about the home life my husband and I would build together. Preparing for a baby by myself taught me something fundamental. I learned that whatever thoughts or ideas I had about relationships were laughably underdeveloped. For the first time in my adult life, I could feel the wool being lifted from my eyes. The realization scared me.

I had a twin brother. His name was Carlyle Jameson Miller. The Lord brought us into this world on August 28, 1983. Heartbreakingly, he went home to be with our Father on November 26, 2020. Carlyle was one of the most remarkable human beings I've ever had the privilege of being bonded with. We were wombmates. We grew up together. We shared a connection that very few people will ever understand. Looking back, my relationship with my twin brother was foundational in how I viewed relationships and what I wanted in a partner. Because he was my favorite person in the whole world and a boy twin, I naturally wanted a companion like my Bro, but because my perspective on the matter was so underdeveloped, I did not realize this until much later in life. I told my now husband when I first met him that Carlyle was a third of my heart. My mother and my future husband held the remaining two-thirds. Today, there is a void in my heart that will never be filled, nor would I want it to be. Carlyle will always occupy that place in my heart until I see him again. I love you, Bro!

My bond with my twin brother is a unique relationship. He was not a child or spouse, but we shared a companionship that a lot of siblings who are close to one another share. The difference was how connected we were, even when we weren't near one another. We naturally stayed in connection with one another. It was an unspoken understanding. It wasn't accidental how our paths took us in different directions, yet our individual life journeys shared a familiar theme.

I never told him who he could or could not date, but we both knew I had to love his spouse, and she had to love me the same. Likewise, my future husband had to bond well with my twin brother. Our future children had to grow up together. No matter what, we had to be a part of each other's lives. We were twins. Enough said.

The day I joined the Navy, I remember driving home and proudly announcing to Carlyle, *"We're joining the Navy! Grab your social security card and birth certificate, and let's go. We're going to the recruiting station."* After a 15-second delay and several slow, awkward blinks later, he simply said, "Okay." That 15-second delay was him processing all that I was committing us to. The slow and awkward blinking was him taking the opportunity to make the moment funny. He grabbed his information and got into the car. I drove right back to the recruiting office with Carlyle. We were starting the journey together. Speaking of funny, in honor of Carlyle, I have to tell you one of the funniest memories of our time together. I'll come back to my relationship point in a moment.

In the Navy, the buildings that housed the recruits in boot camp were called *ships.* Within these ships were groups of recruits who lived and trained together. Each group comprised about 80-90 recruits, called a *division.* My twin brother and I were a part of the same ship but were in different divisions. I was in an all-female division. He was in an all-male division. Within a ship, they're known as brother and sister divisions (ha, there's a pun). Brother and sister divisions often participated in training exercises together but were still distinctly their own division. Within the first week of arriving at boot camp, Carlyle and I were well-acclimated to our new life at training command. One of my favorite training exercises was formation and drilling. My division moved, marched, ran, chanted, and functioned as a unified team. We were sharp! Here's the thing, one of the first rules of drilling is this: Do not break formation! For one, you'll stand out, and everyone will know who the dirtbag was. Secondly, you leave yourself wide open for disciplinary action. Do not break formation! I like rules. I like following rules. I thrive within clear boundaries, structure, and a sense of order. Carlyle and I were twins, but we had our differences.

We celebrated our 19th birthday in boot camp on August 28, 2002. We were drilling in our respective formations that day. I noticed Carlyle's division marching towards mine. We could spot each other as often as our paths crossed, which was often. That day, we both just so happened to be marching on the outside of our three-column division formations. We could have very well brushed shoulders or slapped hands in passing. That's how close we were in proximity. When Carlyle was about 50 feet away, I saw a look in his eyes. He was stoically looking at the back of the person's head directly in front, but I could feel him smirking directly at me on the inside. I KNEW he was going to do something stupid. I felt it in my spirit, and my stomach braced for what he was cooking up in that playful brain of his. Whatever it was, I was not going to like it. I thought to myself. What could Carlyle possibly do in formation, marching, and on our birthday? I didn't have to wait long for the answer. Carlyle did the unspeakable. He broke formation! That man did a gangsta lean out toward me. He uttered in what I guess he thought was a whisper, *"Happy Birthday, Sis."* However, it was loud enough for me to hear over two divisions' marching and singing cadences. He straightened back up and continued marching past me without missing a step. The gangsta lean happy birthday happened in a split second, and I was beyond mortified. Both of our RDCs' (Recruit Division Commanders) saw the formation violation and heard what came out of Carlyle's mouth. Like sharks catching the scent of fresh blood, they had easy prey and immediately went in for the kill. They barked in unison:

Male & Female RDCs: *DIVISIOOOOOOON, HALT!!*

Female RDC: *OOOOOOhhhhhh, is it your birthday Miller?! Well, why didn't you tell me?!*

Male RDC: *Well, well, well, Miller, you didn't tell me you had a sister! And on the same ship!*

Carlyle: *Yes, Petty Officer! She's my twin sister, Petty Officer!*

Female RDC: *HOLY **** How lucky are we?! We have twins on our ship, AND we get to spread some birthday love?!*

Male RDC: *Oh, you done messed up, Miller! It's only fitting that we sing Happy Birthday to the twins!*

Our RDCs' encircled us with at least 160 of our fellow shipmates, ensuring every soul got a good seat for the show. Not only did Carlyle and I get beat (intensive physical exercise) in front of our divisions on what felt like the hottest day that month, but we also got beat again back at the ship later that evening. Our RDCs' called every RDC that was available to our berthing spaces. They wanted to ensure the twins had a proper and memorable birthday. It was more than memorable for me. My Lord, my body was destroyed that day. I was so angry with Carlyle for making me collateral damage for his crazy actions. But low-key, I loved it! It was a pretty freaking awesome birthday. I miss my wombmate.

Relationships. It is a word that can be used

interchangeably with the word *partnership*. The two are seemingly the same, but they have notable differences. A relationship tends to be more personal, mutual, and symbiotic. A partnership has a more contractual connotation. Being in the military taught me more about being in a partnership rather than a relationship. My enlistment was one hundred percent contractual. I pledged my service to the mission of the Navy. If required, I was prepared to die for my country for the sake of freedom. In exchange, the Navy provided me with a living wage, housing, health benefits, and some nice perks. Being the literal person that I am, I took my partnership with the U.S. Navy seriously. Every day, I wanted to be worthy of wearing the uniform. I wanted to represent the Navy well if my face was ever on a billboard. I dedicated a lot of time and energy to be worthy of wearing the uniform. As a holder of various leadership positions, I was committed to exercising my authority in such a manner that honored God, family, and country.

The Navy has a code of conduct that every Marine

and Sailor is required to uphold. I quickly learned that many of those standards reflected my own personal constitution. There was very little anyone could ask of me that I didn't already require of myself. Because of my personal standards, I thrived and enjoyed the military lifestyle. However, as dedicated as I was in my partnership with the Navy, I struggled to balance motherhood, college, career paths, and maintaining somewhat of a social life. There were a lot of nights that I cried over the overwhelming pressure of juggling it all. I was in my twenties. Those were the years to be young and have fun. Instead, I was dealing with some heavy responsibilities, responsibilities most young people do not experience until well into their 30s. I was what the Navy called a greenside Corpsman. Sometimes, people forget that the Marines are a part of the Department of the Navy. Corpsmen provide medical services for our fighting forces. I was in one of those specialties that wore the Marine uniform, went through similar (if not the same) training, and was required to uphold the U.S. Marine Corps standards like the devil dogs I served alongside. Marines and their Corpsmen have a special bond that few truly understand. We are brothers and sisters in arms. You do not talk crap about a Corpsman to a Marine unless you want to get your head bit off. I wish you would say something about one of my Marines. I love my Marines. It is a partnership that I will always cherish.

I have always had a deep need for loyalty and faithfulness in my relationships. It isn't a desire. It's a need. The two words have a significant meaning to me, and it didn't matter the type of relationship or how it was formed. Years of military service and single motherhood helped me set very clear standards for myself and the kind of relationships I chose to engage in. For those reasons, dating life was a struggle. Well, dating was more annoying for me than anything else. I had no problems making friends or maintaining healthy connections with co-workers, but I struggled to find a partner who was just as committed to making our union thrive as I was. Men would say the words that every woman wanted to hear but could not deliver on a fraction of what came out of their mouths. I detested the dating games. The time it took to sift through the wolves and clowns was exhausting. Every man who wanted to date me first needed to distort my seemingly high standard for relationships in order to reduce whatever we did with our time to pure sport and pleasure. Men were smitten with me but unwilling to go the distance and commit to being a father for Machiah or a friend and husband to me. What a waste of time and energy. Yuck!

My unmet need for loyalty and faithfulness was intertwined in other relationships. I've had the pleasure of meeting some of the most amazing women in my lifetime. Women I admired, respected, and who inspired me. Like-minded women, whom I viewed as sisters, often became disingenuous and distant. I've known some supervisors who have had the privilege of working with stellar junior employees who could outperform the masses. Yet, those same supervisors sat back and reaped the benefits of their junior employees' hard labor without giving credit to where it was due.

Likewise, in the marriages I observed, I witnessed spouses who rode the coattails of their significant other's hard work and success with no intention of contributing to the upkeep of the marriage or home life. I've met so many women who held down the fort to support their man's personal and professional goals, only to get the short end of the stick when it was time to pay it forward. Likewise, I've met some extraordinary men and single dads, in and out of uniform, who would do anything for their children. Unfortunately, these men were entangled with contentious, bitter women who made it their personal mission to create drama and strife.

These are just a few examples of poor relationships and a lack of partnership. The value we place on relationships these days is seriously missing the mark. A sense of partnership is almost thoughtless. All of which confused me to no end. I constantly questioned what defined love, a relationship, a partnership, unity, or a vow. Ultimately, I wanted lasting friendships, positive work relations, and lasting intimate bonds. I desired to be the best version of myself in relationships where my partners could do the same. I needed healthy relationships where the well-being of all parties involved was a priority to everyone. I'm not describing a relationship in terms of perfection or absolutes, but a tangible and consistent togetherness. A clear balance in the intentionality to grow together, learn, build, and cultivate something meaningful and life-giving. When it came to friendships, I realized that after years of doing life together, I didn't really know who my friends were. I found myself in so-called friendships that didn't make it past friendly conversations and the occasional meetups to shop and share a meal. Superficial. Anyone who knows me knows that I love investing in my relationships. I'm always open to intellectually stimulating conversations, cheerleading the goals and dreams of loved ones, learning my friend's worldviews and passions, sharing frustrations, and laughing about goofy stuff. For me, it gives my interactions depth and meaning. Sadly, most of my interactions lately have been like a brick wall of political correctness and awkwardly restrained conversations. Even if I tried to create more meaningful depths in my friendships, it was clear I was not welcome to be more than a friendly casual acquaintance. I asked myself over the years if I was asking too much from the people I loved and respected. Do I hold too high a standard on relationships that couldn't possibly be met? I questioned my value in relationships and whether I was worthy of what I was asking from others. These were thoughts that I wrestled with, but I had never taken the time to find a viable solution or peace to my dilemma. That is, until my twin brother died. I later came to the understanding that I was asking more of my family and friends than they were willing or able to give. I gave more than what was asked and waited in vain for it to be reciprocated. The problem, as it turned out, was me.

Have you ever tried to discuss an attitude or behavior problem you had with a supervisor, friend, or loved one where their response was, "I don't see anything wrong with it" or "you're the only one that seems to have a problem," or "everything is fine the way it is." After years of scratching my head trying to figure out why the people around me were okay with mediocre and substandard relations, I made a profound discovery. Their words were absolutely true. You see, my relationships and partnerships, with the exception of my husband, were remarkably consistent over the years. I knew my friends and family loved me and demonstrated their love the best way they were able to or even wanted to. They weren't acting funny or changing on me. I was changing. The epiphany was like an explosion went off in my mind. I was changing. I was evolving. Like a tree that you can't see growing, you just look up one day and notice how much it has grown. I'd always strive to be a better version of myself year after year but never stopped to consider if I would recognize myself after a significant amount of time had passed. We preach growth and maturity yet hold on to the same picture of ourselves in our minds. By the time I was 25, there was a stark difference between that 18-year-old pregnant girl. The year I turned 30, I married the sweetest man I'd ever known. I was notably a better version of my 20-something-year-old self. As I approach 40, I've never felt more powerful or had more clarity about who I am. I'm ready to live my best life all over again. The problem was I (here goes the "e" word) expected my relationships to naturally mature and evolve as I did.

Subconsciously, I assumed my friendships and family relations would organically grow with me. Oh, how wrong I was in that line of thinking. As innocent as the notion was, I cannot rush another person's life journey or expect it to go in the same direction as mine. Embarrassing as it was, I had to take a big bite of humble pie and chew on the arrogance and vanity of that line of thinking. Afterwards, I was left with the problem of not having a sense of fulfillment in my relationships. I was lacking. For a long time, I never considered where that lack was coming from. I was happy to have a casual friend and grateful that my loved ones were around to hang out with from time to time. Again, that is, until Carlyle died.

Ironically, I had a physical and mental breakdown

eight months before he died. You can call it mommy exhaustion, a lack of self-care, or severe depression. All I knew was that I broke mentally and physically. In March 2020, I checked myself into a veteran's medical treatment facility; crying, head pounding, confused and completely lost. I was not suicidal, nor did I want to do self-harm. However, I could no longer see the purpose and value in life. I didn't want to be on this earth any longer. Physically, I did not want to do life anymore. Mentally, nothing in my life made sense, and I could no longer reason my way out of that line of thinking. My life no longer had meaning or purpose. I asked myself over and over, *why am I even here? What is the point?* My twin brother took his life on Thanksgiving Day, November 2020. Typical of how my mind works, when something challenges my reality, how I understand things to be, or when I discover things that are out of the ordinary, my brain needs to rectify the *how and why*. How and why did it happen? At the time, his wife had just returned from a long deployment and soon after she was called out of state for training. I knew it was stressful on Carlyle, being married, yet having to function in a single-parent role while your spouse was away for months at a time. I didn't want to add to that stress by sharing my mental health struggles. We talked almost every day, but I suppose neither of us wanted to share what we were struggling with for the same reasons. Did the pressures of life burn him out? Did I not support him enough? Did he know the degree to which his actions would devastate the family? Sadly, I'll never have closure with the *how* and *why*, but coupled with the non-fatal events that happened to me earlier that year, it forced me to take a major step back and begin examining my own *how and whys.* It took nearly 18 months of therapy to discover how vital healthy relationships and partnerships are for me. You can say they're almost like my lifeline. I attributed superficiality and inconsistencies in my relationships to my mental and physical pain. I blamed only one person for what I went through in early 2020, me. I am not in the habit of relying on other people to provide for me, something God has already given and equipped me with. However, we are relational beings. I am wired to be relational. From my relationship with my mother to the connection I share with my neighbors, I was designed for authentic and life-giving relations. When we don't treat our relationships and partnerships with value and invest in them, it does something to a person. It's a form of isolation. I believe prolonged isolation is unnatural and a form of cruelty. I know I am meant to be in healthy, fulfilling, life-giving relationships. When that design is devalued or neglected, I found out in 2020 how it directly affects me.

Lions & Lionesses

When I think of child-rearing, I picture a pride of lions. A play on words circles in my head with all sorts of imagery. For me, a family is similar to a pride. Children are the young lions and lionesses that we're called upon to raise and teach how to thrive in a wild and chaotic world. Men are the leaders and protectors. Women are powerful, fierce, and, when necessary, ruthless. My view of womanhood stems from my mother, grandmother, women in the church, servicewomen, and life experiences. My entrance into womanhood started as a 19-year-old single mother. Even at that time in my life, my son Machiah was like a young cub to me. I've always viewed my man-child as someone who would grow up to be a strong-willed and capable young man, powerful in his own right. A man who will one day walk in his God-given purpose is not easily lured into cultural norms and isn't afraid to stand alone if need be. When I began writing this book, my son was 18 years old and everything I hoped to see in a young man. He was a labor of love and a joy to watch grow into manhood. He still has a lot to navigate through in this life, but I couldn't be prouder of the foundation paved for him.

My Hubby, Brandon, and I have four daughters and no biological sons together. I've noticed that with men, there is a sense of duty in raising young boys that is different from their fervor for raising daughters. In many ways, how a young man carries himself reflects the intentionality of his father's investment in him. However, the intentionality fathers have towards rearing their young daughters has always been skewed from my vantage point. There are subtle, if not blatant, differences I have witnessed since I was an 8-year-old girl that I could not articulate until I had daughters of my own. Brandon taught and modeled the many roles and responsibilities of a man, a husband and father. He wanted to ensure Machiah knew what it meant to be a man. He has always held the belief that fathers (and father figures) were charged with ushering boys into manhood. Men who made the intentional choice to actively engage in the role of fatherhood have the honored privilege of sending their boys out into the world, carrying their father's seal of approval with them. A seal that says, this young man is a reflection of my intentionality and commitment as a man. God had a different plan for Brandon and I. We have been blessed with four beautiful mocha chocolate girls. How Brandon operates as a girl-dad hasn't always been as it is now. Initially, there was a shortage in the intentionality department. His time, attention, efforts, and sense of purpose were less consistent than when Machiah was younger. My nephew, Emerson, is a few years older than our twin daughters. Emerson has the type of personality any man would love to pour and mold into manhood. He's highly inquisitive, contemplative, eager to learn, and listens attentively to every word that comes out of your mouth. He also loves to spend quality time just hanging out with family and talking; he is a treasure to be around. Brandon is a natural teacher. He loves to explain things to the most minute detail and often lingers on the same point longer than humanly necessary. He and Emerson are two peas in a pod. They can geek out for hours about anything and everything. When Brandon teaches Emerson how to wield an ax or explains why the ocean tides move in the direction they do, Brandon has absolute sunshine in his eyes. When those two intellectually bond, it is something special to witness.

Hubby loves chopping wood. I have no idea why he likes it so much, but he enjoys wielding an ax and splitting wood. Emerson lived with us for a brief period of time after my brother died. The months following Carlyle's death in November 2020 were a rough transition for all of us. We naturally formed a support system to encourage one another during our time of grief. Brandon, of course, was accommodating and happy to have a young man in the house. Machiah moved out the year prior, so the ratio of testosterone to estrogen was laughably off balance in our house. With Emerson around, he once again had a buddy to share in all the many things he enjoyed doing. Brandon worked the third shift at a hospital at the time. He drove an hour to and from work five days a week. Regardless of how tired he was, he would spend a few hours with Emerson when he got home on Friday mornings. They did lawn maintenance, tinkered in the garage, and chopped wood. Emerson was his right-hand man on Friday mornings. He intentionally and consistently spent quality time with Emerson doing memorable activities. Time is precious. No one knows how much time they have in this life. How we spend our time matters. Best believe, Hubby enjoyed his time with Emerson on those Friday mornings. In a young boy's mind, I would imagine Emerson felt special and, as I would imagine, developed a sense of worthiness because of his uncle's time and attention. One Friday morning, when Brandon arrived home from work, he jumped out of the truck and walked straight to the garage to set up his lawn equipment. Emerson met his Uncle Brandon in the driveway, ready to hang out. My oldest daughter, Autumn, just so happened to run outside to greet her Dada and ask if she could chop wood with them. As soon as Brandon saw her running toward the equipment laid out in the driveway, he gestured for her to return to the house and gently explained how she needed to wait for another time to work with Dada. Emerson and Hubby were already dawning their safety gear in preparation and did not want Autumn to get hurt while his focus was strictly on teaching Emerson how to handle an ax and chainsaw. As reasonable and well-intended as that sounded, it was clear that Autumn walked away completely let down, as if she was a nuisance. I quickly asked Brandon if Autumn could at least sit and watch so that next time, she'd know the rules to working with Dada in the yard. Her face lit up in hopeful excitement. She had a twinkle in her eyes and was eager to participate, even if that meant simply sitting on the truck and taking mental notes. Of course, Brandon obliged. Later that evening, during my alone time, I considered what kind of imprint interactions, like what happened in the garage, could leave on a young and impressionable girl's mind. Autumn is a lot like her mommy. Observant, analytical, contemplative, and a processor. I am also a realist. I'd rather call a situation for what it is rather than create a reality in my mind that I'm comfortable living in. In my experience, it is much easier to take the ugly truth of reality and complement it rather than live in the delusion of one's own making. A girl's impression of how her father perceives her matters tremendously. Later that evening, Brandon and I discussed how we, as parents, communicate our affections to our children and how our day-to-day mannerisms affect their self-worth. Our actions and verbal communication with our children have to be intentional. This is especially true when it comes to a father's interactions with his daughter. I want nothing more than for all my nieces, nephews, sons, and daughters to feel equally empowered, worthy, valued and not feel pressured to conform to cookie-cutter social norms. It is evident in how I've always aspired to create a home environment where my children, and any child in my sphere of influence, have the space to grow into fierce lions and lionesses; men and women who complement one another with their strengths and abilities.

When Brandon is talking about history and passing on tidbits of information to our nephews, you can see his eyes beam with pride (ha, ha, another pun). However, when it came to our daughters, there was a different light in his eyes. Perhaps it dimmed when Machiah moved out. The twins were five years old and just becoming more interactive with what Hubby and I did around the house. Emerson was at an age where he asked more thought-provoking questions and willingly listened to adult feedback. In hindsight, neither of us immediately recognized the shift happening in that particular season of child-rearing. After all, there was so much change and transition happening with our family dynamic. The passion wasn't as fervent when reading to Avigail or talking Apphia out of her regular toddler temper tantrum. The time and intentionality rarely stretched on for longer than what was required with our daughters. It was so subtle I could have easily brushed it off as the routine grind of life and paid it no mind. However, after some time, I began to notice it more frequently, whatever *it* was. Over time, and with much thought and observation, I formulated how to talk with Hubby about what I identified as a disparity. One of the many things I love about the man God gave me, is Brandon's constitution. He has a strong heart for family and justice. From the moment he met Machiah, he has treated him like his own. We would have loved to have a set of twin mocha chocolate boys, but God gave us different blessings; four beautiful daughters. Side note, we don't always recognize answered prayers when our blessings come in packaging we didn't imagine they would come in. I've learned that God gives us exactly what we want and need before we even know it for ourselves. It is funny how we thank God when a need is met, but when we don't recognize an answered prayer as the blessing we have been waiting for, we question or overlook it. When a bill is overdue, and an unexpected check comes in the mail, it's immediately realized as a blessing. We're so thankful for it. When a man deeply desires a son, yet pink confetti explodes out of a balloon at the gender reveal party, he tries his best to mask the physical reaction of disappointment. I chuckle to myself

44

each time I remember the moments Brandon found out he was having girl after girl after girl after girl. When I was 25, I was extremely discontent with being single, hadn't had a real relationship in years, and was nowhere close to being married and having a family. In my season of singleness, I could not see how the waiting period was a huge blessing for me.

My concern with the disparity in intentionality towards our four daughters isn't malicious. I'm grateful to Brandon for stepping in to foster Machiah into manhood. I'm thankful to be married to a man who takes pride (hehe, pun) in modeling affirming manhood for our son and nephews. Brandon honors my late brother in ways words could not express. The disparity concern for my four daughters was not that they were getting less attention from their Dada. It was about how they would remember the moments Dada could have drawn them closer yet sidelined them. Will they question their value? As minuscule as it may seem, it greatly affects how little girls view themselves. After all, I am a woman. I do have an inside perspective on the matter. Many women with a father present in the home can attest to how it felt to be slighted by their father's affections. I grew up with an older brother, my twin brother, and baby sister. Carlyle and I were the middle children. I was an AB honor student. For the most part, I kept my nose clean and wanted to please my parents. Carlyle was that middle child that did not need much, didn't complain, and could easily be overlooked because he was so quiet. My baby sister was the master of hiding in plain sight. She lived under the radar and only surfaced when necessary. To this day, Me'ghen is the fly on the wall who gets a kick out of people-watching. My oldest brother, Brandon (yes, my husband and brother have the same first name), had a particular affinity for getting in trouble. He got a lot of attention with all the shenanigans he was into. Carlyle and I got into very little trouble, so Mom and Dad didn't need to be hands on with us. We were on autopilot. Me'ghen was the baby. The baby ALWAYS receives the most positive attention. Not that I'm jealous or anything. My oldest brother probably got more attention than the three of us combined. Whether he wanted it or not, positive or negative, he got intentional time and attention.

My parents have been married for over 35 years. Both were prior Army, so you best believe discipline was very present, and punishments were handed out swiftly in our household. Both could equally be the judge, jury, and executioner. "When your father gets home..." threats never came out of my mother's mouth. When we got in trouble, there was no need to wait until Dad got home. Mom handled that just fine. When my father got home, he had the option of putting the disciplinary cherry on top. My siblings and I laugh about it to this day. The point is they both were hard-working folks and good parents. No parent is perfect. We all have our shortcomings. That's part of being human. Of all the possible areas parents could miserably fail, every parent has that one area where failure is not an option. For me, I want all my children to understand their worth and value. I hope I do them justice in that endeavor. I need them to understand their value because I know how the world will try to convince them otherwise. Children are easily impressed upon. They soak up the information around them and shape their perspectives through experiences. What they come to know and understand to be true in this world will be filtered through various mediums. It will challenge them as men and women and shape their identities. They'll have to wrestle through these challenges. How they view themselves and understand their purpose sets the stage for the type of men and women they will be in this world. The fathers of daughters play an unimaginably massive role during a young girl's journey into womanhood.

I asked Hubby one day, out of the blue, what imagery pops up in his mind when he thinks about a pride, its purpose and how they function. It's typical for people to conjure up imagery from *The Lion King*. I instantly picture a pack of lions lying around in a den (pun intended). Look! I am going to adopt a code word for these fantastic puns; {pineapple!}. When you see {Pineapple!}, appreciate my puns. Here's a question:

How many large thick maned lions are in a pride? How many lionesses? The imagery is so powerful in my mind because I understand the importance of its design and each lion's role. They are different yet complementary in nature {pineapple!}. Every lion plays a role toward the well-being of the whole. I've always desired my family unit to function similarly. I am encouraged by the analogy of a pride, mainly {pineapple!} because of the lionesses. I have a house full of girls who have yet to discover their purpose, talents, strengths, or how they will make their mark in this world. Hubby and I are teaching our girls to be fierce. We have told them since they were old enough to understand that they are mighty warriors. Those seeds are most definitely producing good fruit. When my girls can't figure something out, I often hear them say to themselves, "I can do this! I'm a mighty warrior!" It always makes my heart smile.

Machiah was about 13 years old when I transitioned from active-duty service. Hubby was still in the Navy pursuing a special warfare program in Panama City,

Florida. The kids and I followed him there. He was confined to the Navy Surface Warfare Center while in training. We lived roughly seven miles away in an apartment complex, yet we rarely saw him. I was juggling our one- year-old twin daughters and a teenager. We settled into our little apartment and quickly set a routine for ourselves. Homeschool during the day, church on Wednesdays and Sundays, and as much family fun as we could fit in between. Things were going great for the first 30 days. However, I was beginning to feel overwhelmed towards the middle of month two. I needed a break from the routine, and some much-needed adult fun. Life revolved around toddlers and teenage confusion. One particular Sunday morning, my heart was heavy. I woke up overwhelmed and frustrated. Trying to prepare everyone for an early morning Bible study group was a lot. I loved my Bible study group on Sunday mornings. I could geek out on theology for hours. One of my Master of Arts degrees is in Theology. Those were the best 18 months of college work I had ever done and probably will ever do. Trying to make it to a 9:00 am Bible study on time was quite a task with three children. Preparing breakfast, minor clean-up, getting dressed, packing diaper bags, and getting myself ready was a full-blown evolution, as they say in the Navy. I made it on time each Sunday but was often exhausted when I dropped all the kids off in their Sunday school classroom. The walk to the Bible study classroom was like climbing out of a pool. I felt so incredibly heavy, physically and mentally. Usually, when I arrived at Bible study, I would fix a cup of tea and have a pastry that a member of the group so thoughtfully prepared. Best of all, I could enjoy some social time with other adults. It lifted my spirits. That particular Sunday, I was rushing to prepare for church in an absolute frenzy. One of the twins produced a massive blowout. It seeped out of her diaper, up her back, and through her clothes. I smelled it when I finished packing the diaper bag and was about to walk out the door. I had to stop everything, strip her down, wash and change her clothes. Machiah was in a funky mood that morning {pineapple!}. Occasionally, he'd wake up and decide he didn't want to listen to his mother and kinda-sorta obeyed what was asked of him. That brotha was riding a thin line between procrastination and straight-up disobedience that Sunday, and I was not having it. He must have forgotten who his mama was. This mama ain't afraid to put her Bible down and handle business. After a couple of rounds of back and forth talking back, not listening, and dragging his lazy butt about, I decided we weren't going to Bible study that morning. I gave the twins a snack and set them on the living room floor to play. For the next hour or so, Machiah and I sat down to try and map out exactly where he had lost his mind and figure out how to get him back into his right mind.

By the time we finally arrived at church, I was more overwhelmed than most Sundays. Taking the time to talk with your children when they act out can weigh heavily on the spirit. It is hard work. When children, especially teenagers, lose their minds, it takes an enormous amount of self-control not to knock 'em back into their right minds. I sat down in the church pew that morning, fighting back the tears. Machiah was chatting it up with his buddies on the other side of the sanctuary. I felt myself just staring off into the distance. I couldn't tell you what was in front of my eyes, only that I stared straight ahead. I was processing the events of the morning and contemplating this thing called motherhood so deeply that I literally couldn't see what was in front of me. While teary-eyed and lost in my thoughts, a lady from my Bible study group walked over to say hello. She asked how I was doing and said she missed me during morning Bible study. I'm not the type of person who will say, "oh, I'm fine, and you?" when asked about my well-being. I'm usually uncomfortably honest and direct. *"Giiiirl, I'm bout to cry. It's been a rough morning. One of the twins pooped so much that it went out her diaper and up her back, and my son needed a serious parenting moment this morning, so I decided to skip Bible study. I'm tired. I need a break."* Just then, I thought about the raspberry Danishes one member of our Bible study group brought every 3rd Sunday. It was the 3rd Sunday! Raspberry Danishes are one of my favorite breakfast delights. Grrr! I missed fellowship, Danishes, a hot cup of tea, conversation with grown-ups, and "me time!" That's when the tears broke free. Unfortunately, the poor lady who fell into my pity party froze for a good 10 seconds. She stared at me with eyes wide open, shaking her head up and down slowly. I don't think she expected an honest answer, nor was she prepared to respond. She said, *"I understand. You'll get through this, hun,"* and gave me a couple of "attaboy" pats on my knee. In that instant, and through my tears, I gave her a more in-depth explanation of how I was doing:

"You know what it is? I am raising a lion. Sometimes I lose sight of the fact that he is still a cub. He is all over the place with his mood, attitude, and communication skills. I see him as the man I know God has called him to be, and I sometimes forget that he is still a growing man-child. He's very aware and intelligent for his age, but he's still a snot-nosed child who can be a real jerk, you know? It reminds me that lions are apex predators. Cubs are raised in the wild. With young men, there can be

a sort of ferociousness in their development that, if we as mothers aren't paying attention, can disconnect us from the bigger picture. God has plans and purposes for Machiah. It's my job to be patient with him and guide him toward discovering that purpose, whatever it may be. I got scratched and clawed this morning, but it was my fault. I get so busy trying to keep a schedule and fixated on the routines of life that I forget my purpose. I'm raising a lion and lionesses. Some days are going to be rough. On other days we will straight up have to brawl. But I can't forget why God gave me that little man-child."

I looked at the lady, forgetting I was talking to another person. In hindsight, I was ministering to my spirit and talking through the chaos in my head. She smiled politely and said, "that's good, honey." Again, she was not prepared for a response. Side note: it irks me how people, especially church folks, ask how you're doing but don't care to know. It's like a thing you say when we see each other. It's weird to me how someone can approach me and ask, "how are you doing?" and not be prepared for an actual response. The interaction wasn't meant to go beyond the question and a default answer. Anyway, the lady walked away, and I continued to sift through my thoughts. It made me feel better to put the chaos in my spirit into words. It wasn't that a poopy diaper inconvenienced me, that I missed those amazing raspberry danishes, or even my disrespectful teenager. I realized that I was wonderfully & overwhelmingly burdened with God's plan for my children. Somedays, that reminder catches me off guard, but it always has a way of centering me back into the right perspective. Looking back, I am so proud of those moments. They hurt at the time, but the memory of how they worked out overshadows the temporary growing pains. I realized those moments with my then 13-year-old son helped me to be more patient and intentional with my daughters. There is a considerable age gap between my son and the girls. In that gap of time {pineapple!}, my perspective on motherhood matured significantly. Today, when my daughters act out, I have much more clarity and understanding of how God works in real time. I look back at Machiah's upbringing as a reference and can respond more constructively when my girls act out.

As I reflect on how much I've grown as a parent, I also think about Hubby's growth. Hubby can now recognize the disparities in how he allots his time and attention and communicates his affection. He is much more intentional as a girl dad and male role model. He invites my daughter into activities he enjoys, usually chopping wood, tinkering in the garage, and building projects. I rolled my eyes the day he came home all excited with four hot pink toolbox kits from Lowe's. Classic girl dad. He has transitioned into a fantastic girl dad and found passion in teaching, empowering, and validating our little lionesses. He chops wood with Apphia, geeks out with Autumn, creates mind-twisting stories with Alexis Nevaeh, and can play memory card games with two-year-old Avigail for hours. My hope is that when these girls are older, they will look back over their lives and recognize how important those moments were, how they contributed towards their self-worth and value as women, and how blessed they are for it.

Self-Criticism & Destructive Thinking

You are so dumb. How could you let that happen? There is no going back if you mess this up. He'll never love you. You don't deserve her. She hates me! Mom doesn't have time for you. Dad doesn't care. Why are you bothering her? Just give up. Let it go. You're wasting your time. They're all laughing at you. No one respects you. What's the point?

I know a lot of people who torment themselves with self-criticism. These are the same people plagued with a destructive thought life that manifests into hostile and dysfunctional behavior and speech patterns. I understand how easily a mistake, thoughtless comment, or someone's seemingly unfavorable facial reaction can throw a person into a downward spiral of embarrassment, shame, disappointment, or fear. I can relate to that burning feeling of disgust thinking about a past action or comment, how I was let down or felt unworthy of a person's time, attention, and affection. Thoughts and feelings of self-hate can play like a broken record in our minds. My mind can recall and fester memories of the cruel things I said, something I did that hurt someone I loved or moments when someone else had to reap the consequences of my poor choices. I can be so hard on myself, criticizing every word that comes out of my mouth or every deed that results in embarrassment. As hard as I try to stay positively oriented and engaged in constructive thinking, these thoughts inevitably creep into my psyche. It's like they come out of nowhere. I could be helping my daughter with her math homework when, in the middle of regrouping an equation when a replay of an argument I had with a friend from years ago pops up and takes center stage in my mind. I can relive those tumultuous moments and feel just as badly as if the moment happened yesterday. Likewise, Brandon and I could be out shopping, laughing, and having a great afternoon when I suddenly recall some stupid thing I said in front of a hundred people. Those moments frustrate me. It's like simultaneously living in the past and present. I'd much rather live in the present and actively think of my future.

Hubby can attest to battling with self-criticism and destructive patterns of thought. It usually occurs while he's at work cleaning surgical instruments in a decontamination room. Monotonous work is an open field for an idle mind to wander. Hubby can fester in self-hate and criticism for hours and go deeper and deeper into that pit for reasons he can't explain. Some people are better at talking their way out of pits of torment or redirecting their thoughts to something more constructive, while others need a little more help and practice getting there. It wasn't until I had a complete mental and physical breakdown that I decided to consciously put all those bad memories and self-torments in their final resting place. I needed to be set free from the mental and emotional strongholds. My spirit needed resting peace and to know that I am loved, worthy, and forgiven for my sins. I needed to walk in newness with the assurance that no matter what I did or said moving forward, it would not have such a long-lasting effect on me. I was beyond tired of carrying the weight of past mistakes and failures. I also could not afford to bring shame, disappointment, and a self-defeating thought life into my future. There was no place for it. I was tired of constantly reliving feelings of sorrow, going out of my way to earn the approval of others, or trying my hardest not to step on anyone's toes. Like constantly apologizing, giving "I'm sorry" gifts, and being overly polite would magically make everything better, and I wouldn't have a negative feeling or thought about myself. The bottom line is I needed to create balance internally. I knew I had the propensity to be hard on myself and scrutinize everything I said or did. Although I knew I was not perfect, I was not living that truth. The self-criticism needed to be dealt with.

The year I started my business, I saw immense potential and success in my future. However, I couldn't see a future that I wanted to live in with loads of unresolved mental and emotional garbage hanging over my head. I first needed to rid myself of the self-inflicted cage I unconsciously found myself in. I recognized I needed to be released from any obligation to be more than who I was, learn to be kind to myself, and demand that same kindness from others. Next, I needed to practice being my unapologetic and authentic self. Instead of compromising what I knew to be true about my identity, in order for others to feel comfortable with the bold and passionate spirit God gave me, I had to learn to be okay with distancing myself from certain relationships. As put-together as I may appear, I wrestle with anger, disappointment, and feelings of unworthiness. I was always too much, too bold, too forward, too strong, too aggressive...the list is not exhaustive. Suppressing all that I knew to be powerful and great within me manifested into anger, resentment, confusion, bitterness, and self-criticism. There were, of course, external sources of criticism and malice that contributed to the broken mindset I'd discovered about myself. Surprisingly, I wasn't as angry towards those situations and peculiar personalities as much as I was disappointed over how I'd compromised what made me unique and powerful. Tumultuous seasons in my life and difficult people fueled me. I manifested all the external criticism and malice projected at me into a ridiculous amount of productivity and success in my personal and professional life. I made it my mission to turn whatever jealousy or malice people held toward me, said about me, or projected on me into a success story. My default response was to rack up awards, accolades, and promotions until I could look back and watch the green envy goblins, negative nancies, and naysayers eat crow. Lest I give too much credit to the mean-spirited person or unfavorable circumstances, it didn't take much for either to push me to succeed in that way. I was already hard on myself. My thought life was worse than anything a man or woman could ever say to my face. I loved myself but could be so unkind to my spirit at the same time. The same could be said about friends, co-workers, and family members wrestling with self-criticism and a destructive thought life. They love dearly but can be so unkind to themselves and others. It took time and intentionality to sort through my anger and self-criticism. I learned to redirect all that negative energy to birth and cultivate constructive passions I could live with. The glory for my deliverance belongs to God alone. However, all the resources in the world could not do the internal work of healing that I needed to do with God's help.

I had an interesting conversation with my then-17-year-old son about self-criticism and destructive thoughts. It was more than a conversation; it was an experience. I witnessed first-hand what self-criticism looked like when my son Machiah and I had a conversation in the laundry room one day. It was like looking into a mirror, and it broke my heart. At that moment, all I wanted to do was speak wisdom and life into a heart enslaved by hate and self-criticism. The kind of wisdom that was always in me, but I had never taken the time to speak it into my own heart. I believe God wired my mind and emotions to see and feel the pains of others. I listen to people's words from their hearts. I may need a reminder of the context of the verbal conversation, but I can write a dissertation about what I felt their heart language was saying to me. Perhaps I could never speak to my own heart because the rattling of self-criticism and the clanging of self-hate drowned out that small voice trying to get my attention.

The day started with guilt over falling behind on some housework and the homeschool schedule. I struggled to be consistent with the girls' lesson plans and keep an organized home. Life, as you know, has a way of throwing you off track. We forget to make room for those unforeseen variables that inevitably throw us curve balls. Then again, sometimes you have to let go, submit to the ride, and simply do your best. As a busy mom, waking up with guilt takes a toll on my day. It was about eight o'clock in the morning. I usually do self-care in my bedroom before I open my door to face the day. I like to shower, stretch, and set my intentions for the day. It helps me take those first thoughts when I wake up and, if needed, re-frame them before I open the door to screaming children. When I came out of my room that particular day, I remember thinking, not again. The hallway had piles of dirty clothes lined up for at least 20 feet. When you wake up in the morning with residual chores from the day prior, it puts a damper on the day. I feel a setback emotionally. Whatever motivation I had mustered up behind closed doors deflated a little. The usual dinosaurs, books, and unicorns magically climbed out of their bins, off the shelves, and onto the floor during the night. They tended to make their way out of the girls' rooms and onto the middle hallway for me to see when I opened my bedroom door. It was a mess. Any parent committed to the work at home knows that housework carried over from the day prior compounds the work for the following day. Time is not kind to the stay-at-home parent on those days. There were many days when I kissed my husband off to work at 7:30 am. Then, after what felt like a few hours, he came through the front door. I would ask in a panic, "What are you doing at home?! Did something happen at work? Did you get fired?!" Laughably, I didn't realize eight hours had gone by. Brandon was conditioned on those days to settle and reassure me with the simple words, "Honey, I've been at work for eight hours. You seem a little overwhelmed. How can I be of service?"

It was a Monday morning. I asked my tall, handsome son to do the laundry the day before. At age 17, my man-child knew the way I liked things. He is required to contribute to the household if he isn't enrolled in school full-time and/or is unemployed. So daily, I give him tasks that help our home life function more smoothly. If he chooses to go above and beyond what is asked, it's a huge blessing to his Mama. Occasionally, my man-child would fall into a behavior pattern not conducive to maintaining a functioning household— disappearing, doing the bare minimum only when asked, avoiding eye contact and all forms of communication, retreating to the bathroom often, and walking around like a grouch. There have also been occasions when he'd go radio silent for a couple of days. I'd have to open his bedroom door to check if there was still a living body in the room. When he wanted money, a haircut, or a special request, Machiah knew precisely what to do. If my teenager was up and dressed before me, terrifyingly cheerful and ready to be a productive member of the family, he obviously wanted something from me. I asked Machiah to do laundry the previous day. I needed five loads of laundry washed, dried, folded, hung up, and put away. It was the only task for that day. I woke up Monday morning to see the laundry had not magically disappeared off the floor and reappeared in the closets and drawers. Not a problem. Maybe it slipped his mind. I gave him grace. *"Machiah, you forgot the laundry. Get it done today, son."* On Tuesday, when I came out of my room, it was like deja vu. The laundry was still scattered down my hallway. *"Good morning, Machiah. Why didn't you finish the laundry I asked you to do yesterday? Is there a problem?"* Why do teenagers look at you blankly when you ask them simple questions? I honestly can't remember doing that to my parents. My mother would give me such a terrifying stare-down, I'd anxiously give any answer just to relieve myself of her intimidating gaze. It never fails. Teenagers act like it's a trick question and look all confused. My son scratches his head, rubs the back of his neck, takes a couple of long, exaggerated breaths, and looks at the floor. After a good and awkward 15 seconds, I broke the deafening silence. *"Yello? Can I get an answer?"* He replied with the only answer he was willing to say, *"Yes, ma'am."* My voice had a little base in it as I replied, *"Get it done."* Those moments always made me feel gangsta, like Angela Bassett in *Waiting to Exhale*. Bernadine did not play!

I honestly could not explain how Wednesday came and went with no recollection of the day's events. The children were still alive and safe, no property was damaged, and I knew my name. Success. When I woke up that Thursday morning, I was confident that my man-child had completed the task his gracious and loving mother asked him to do. Do you think he did it? Astonishingly enough, he did not touch the laundry. If I had taken a picture of the mess in the hallway on Monday and Thursday, those pictures would be completely identical. The laundry wasn't touched, moved, shuffled, or manipulated. Machiah was standing outside the laundry room door, frozen, looking at me, doing and saying nothing. I was so enraged that I feared I would say something to negatively set the tone for the rest of the day. I wanted to have a good day. The Lord spoke to my heart, saying, *Alexis, go back to your room.* I turned around and gave myself another 10 minutes of self-care.

When I came out of my room, I was ready for battle. Machiah was still in the hallway waiting for me. To my continued surprise, he wasn't scrambling to get the laundry sorted or throwing any of it into the washing machine. He was standing in the same place I'd left him 10 minutes prior, just waiting for me to lose my mind. *"Stop playing with me and get it done, Machiah DeAndre Miller!"* I'm sure I looked like a complete psycho in my fuzzy leopard print robe, mismatched socks, and zebra print bonnet. That joker was lucky. I desperately wanted to have a good day.

Okay, now it's Friday morning. I'm praying on my knees in my bedroom behind closed doors. I would often beg God to allow me to open my bedroom door to the sight of a clean hallway, obedient children greeting me with breakfast on a tray, and all the chores completed. I opened my room door that Friday with my eyes closed. Yes, I literally closed my eyes and opened the door. I stepped out about two feet, then made a left face in the hallway. I opened my eyes. Now, do you think he completed the laundry? It's been four whole God-given days. Surely, Machiah didn't want to invoke the wrath of his sweet Mama on day five. It was Friday, for goodness sake. Who doesn't want to have a happy Friday, right? Nope. I opened my eyes to the same mess I saw Monday through Thursday. Sure, I could have done the laundry and saved myself the headache, but that was not the point. My man-child needed to understand the importance of listening to his parents, obeying what was asked of him, and contributing to the household. I'm willing to let dirty laundry sit in the hallway for a week to ensure the point was drilled into his skull. I opened my son's room door to find him dead asleep, spread out on his bed as if he had just gotten off a 24-hour shift. He was knocked out. Welp, it was now time to go into full nuclear mommy mode. My son received an alarming wake-up call that morning {pineapple!}. My six-foot man-child was jolted out of bed by the voice of what sounded like a fire drill going off directly in his ear. *"Get up! Get your butt up and get my laundry done, NOW!"* Like a drill instructor with nothing but time on my hands, I watched as Machiah dutifully arranged and prepared the laundry for a wash cycle. I served my country for 17 years. Six of which were spent stationed on Navy and Marine recruit training commands. Drilling was one of the fondest memories of my career. Machiah's countenance was angry and confused. Of course, he avoided eye contact and didn't say a word. I could feel the rage steaming out of his head.

Me: *Machiah, I know you just got your butt handed to you, but why are you mad? I should be the only one upset! Carrying on like someone did something so horrible to you isn't an option right now.*

He glanced over and gave me an angry and puzzled look. I shifted into a softer mothering mode with a cooler and much more levelheaded tone about me.

Me: *Machiah, I am not trying to attack you. I need you to understand how big a help you are to me. When you refuse to pull your weight and do your part in our home, it creates a problem that we need to get to the bottom of. What is causing all this anger and discontentment? What is the source of your complete lack of care? I really would like to understand. Can you explain it to me?*

He did not have an answer. He just shrugged his shoulders. Time to dive deeper. I focused all my attention directly into my handsome young man's eyes. I needed to speak directly to his soul, bypassing his emotions, pride, and arrogance. I needed to talk with my son, heart to heart.

Me: *Machiah, if you don't give me something to let me know what's going on in your heart, I can't be here for you or know how to respond. I love you. If this week directly reflects who Machiah Miller is on the inside, anyone would have every reason to assume the worst of you. As your mother and the one who wants the absolute best for you, if this disobedience continues, you leave me* *no room to be there for you in the best way possible. Your body language, tone of voice, and mannerisms... all scream an attitude that is not the son I raised. What I perceive from you is that you're upset, disgruntled, moody, and indifferent. Never mind the disobedience. Your attitude needs to be addressed. Retreating when something is asked of you is not befitting of a king. Preferring to be alone in a dark, smelly room is not the picture of a respectable young man. Demonstrating a complete lack of attention and love for our family is not a man who loves God, himself, his family and others. Do you think it's okay to do the bare minimum and skate by living off other people's hard work and success?*

Once again, the room fell into a deafening silence. This time, I was willing to sit in awkward silence, my attention fixed on his soul, waiting patiently for a response. We stood in the laundry room, facing each other like two dominant personalities playing mental chess. I made my move. It was now his turn to respond. I knew he was processing my words. The mind I nurtured and molded was critically thinking about the claims against his character. Machiah was not one to give fake or superficial verbal responses. Right or wrong, my son was always ready to go to war when called to arms. It felt like minutes had passed. I patiently waited. My heart was broken for him. My spirit was deeply concerned and wanted to understand. I wanted to be there for Machiah, but he had to be the one to open the door. His head shifted down, up at me, and down again periodically. Looking directly into my eyes seems to sear his soul. His breathing sounded heavy. I wanted him to be uncomfortable at that moment. I wasn't going anywhere. I would not interrupt his thought process and would wait all day if needed. He moved, *"can I get back to you on this?"* I quickly and gently responded, *"no,"* without breaking eye contact. One of two things was happening at that moment. He either didn't want to say what needed to be said or was trying to shut me out. The former was more realistic, but my heart was prepared for the latter.

Machiah: *Some days, I wake up feeling like trash. I feel that I'm either doing amazing or horribly. There's nothing in between. No balance. I'm either being helpful, or I'm completely useless. Days when I'm awesome, yea, whatever, it's cool. I'm great, and you guys are always there to say thanks and show your appreciation. Then I forget all that. Some days I wake up feeling like a heaping pile of hot garbage and completely useless.*

Me: *Have I ever made you feel useless or told you that you're worthless?*

Machiah pauses and looks at me curiously, like, 'what kind of a question is that?'

Me: *Think about it. Feel free, to be honest. I can take it.*
Machiah: *No, Mom.*
Me: *Step outside of yourself. Strip away the emotion and pride. Point blank. Do you believe, not think, do you believe what you feel about yourself is the truth or a lie?*

He looked shocked but took the time to think about the question.

Machiah: *No. Not at all.*

Mom: *Let's identify and name the lie. Name it. What thing, person, or situation outside of yourself has given you the impression that you are hot garbage?*

He didn't answer.

Mom: *What in your life has affirmed that you are blessed, special, worthy, and treasured?*

Machiah: *I can name many things, Mom, starting with you.*

Mom: *That tells me that you have allowed these lies to creep into your mind and overrule God's absolute objective truth about who Machiah Miller is. This lie has convinced you to believe that you are garbage. Not only garbage but hot garbage. You chose to believe that lie against all the tangible evidence around you. No one, not family, not friends, or mentors, fed this lie. Name one person who has ever told you or treated you like you were less than or hot garbage.*

Machiah: *No one.*

Mom: *Why have you easily believed a lie about yourself?*

Machiah: *It's true if you think about it. A person is either trash or worth something. You are either useful or useless.*

Mom: *Why, and who says it has to be so extreme? Why can't you be helpful one day and maybe not so helpful another day? Why does not being helpful make you absolutely useless? There may be days when you're not pulling your weight, but it doesn't make you trash.*

Machiah: *I have a right to think what I want to think. We don't have to see eye to eye or agree.*

Mom: *So, if it's a lie, should I just be okay with it and let you sulk in that kind of self-criticism and destructive thinking? Do you expect me to sit back, watch you hate yourself, and not say anything? How does that work exactly?*

Machiah: *It's subjective. Meaning it's how I think, feel or believe.*

Mom: *So, no middle ground? You're either useless or useful.*

Machiah: *Right! I stand by my thoughts.*

Mom: *So, no matter how much I praise you, appreciate you, demonstrate my thanks, tell you how big of a help* *you are to me... you're going to believe that lie?*

Machiah: *Yep!*

Mom: *So, am I lying to myself thinking you have value, set apart, chosen, and a child of the King? Am I lying to you when I remind you of how blessed you are? Am I lying to think that God has a plan for your life, and I can't wait to witness it come to fruition? Am I foolish to pray for you and view you as the man God has created you to be? Not the man-child you are today, but the man who will one day fully recognize the calling over his life to stand, command, and function as a son of the King. Who's the liar Machiah, me or you? It looks like we have two opposing 'truths' here. You believe you are hot garbage. I believe the opposite. Am I the deceptive mother who has been lying to you your whole life? Convincing you that you're something you're not?*

Machiah takes a hard step back. A fight has broken out inside of him, and he's processing it all at once.

Machiah: *Everyone has a right to think what they want.*

Mom: *That is another lie. Everybody has a responsibility* *to weigh their thoughts! Consider what is true and live in reality no matter how it makes you feel or how unpopular or challenging it may be. We all have an intellectual and emotional responsibility to stand for what is true. If you know in your heart that you are not garbage, you are tasked with commanding your thoughts and feelings to expel the lie and live the truth. Convincing yourself of a lie will only create conflict and stress inside of you. That conflict will inevitably spew out and wreck you, your loved ones, and any potential relationship you'd like to have. Am I useless, Machiah?*

My child looks at me with a painful stare. His eyes were swelling up with tears. His hands balled up into tight fists, shoulders raised as if it took his entire body to hold back his tears.

Mom: *According to what you think and believe, people are either useless or useful. There is no variance, spectrum, middle ground, or gray area. If that is true, then we're all useless hot garbage because we are imperfect beings. No one gets it right all the time. We all* *make mistakes and miss the mark. Sometimes we don't feel like being on our A game. Sometimes we do fall into unproductive patterns and seasons of laziness. By your standards, that makes us all useless. If you stand by your 'truth' look me in my eyes and tell me I am a useless mother. I am a useless person. If that is what you believe, tell me to my face.*

Machiah fell speechless. Blank. Completely without words or thought.

Mom: *If we judged the world by your standards, we'd all be in trouble. Nobody is 100% useful all the time, son. So, by default, everyone is useless.*

Pause. Breathe. Relax. Pivot.

Mom: *Machiah, choose to begin respecting yourself more. Don't trash yourself internally. It's not necessary. Yes, everyone has a right to their own opinion. Yes, everyone has a right to believe what they choose to believe if you think that's okay. However, you do not have the right to think poorly of yourself and convince others*

82

to think poorly of you. It's cruel, Honey. If you can't complete a task or you miss the mark, you don't get to have a nasty attitude. There is a better way to deal with these types of problems. Avoidance is a temporary solution. It will only make the inevitable harder to face. Accountability is almost always the answer. Train your heart to confront what's going on inside. It's uncomfortable but necessary. Be honest with yourself. If you lie to yourself long enough, you begin to mold your perspective around a bunch of lies and displace yourself from what is accurate and true. As your mother, it is my job to get under your skin and challenge you. I'm willing to look past that smoke screen and look for the heart of the matter. The heart of the matter is that you're not holding yourself accountable for your actions. Instead, you distract yourself from taking accountability through self-criticism and destructive thinking. Worst of all, you're trying your hardest to convince me that everything you say is true and I'm the liar.

At that moment, Machiah must have temporarily

forgotten who his Mama was. I don't revel in confrontation. It's just as uncomfortable for me as the next person. I get anxious knowing I have to go to war and face conflict. However, I understand that resting peace requires being transparent and authentic. It's ironic how the word *parent* is in transparent. It took time to comprehend fully, but an 'AC pearl of wisdom' was created in the laundry room that day. Since 2020, I have had to make a conscious effort to confront my feelings and thoughts daily. From the moment I wake up, it's like stepping onto a battlefield in my mind, body, and emotions. When those insecurities, doubts, and destructive self-talk creep in, I'm faced with a choice. Either fall into a pit or challenge each thought with the truth of who God says I am. I've repeatedly taught Machiah these concepts at age-appropriate levels throughout his life. It was my hope these concepts would ring true for him one day. He had a lot to think about that day in the laundry room. Witnessing him wrestle through his thoughts and how he viewed himself was painful. I also understood how critical the process was. I couldn't do the work for him. I just had to wait and patiently meet him on the other side.

Machiah: *Thank you, Mom. I'm going to think about all this.*

Mom: *Thank you for listening. I'm here if you need me. Now, get my laundry done!*

Sometime later, Machiah came downstairs to meet me in the kitchen. He sat at the kitchen table. I knew he needed space to prepare to respond to our conversation in the laundry room and I did not want to interrupt or distract him at the moment. I played it cool and continued to keep myself busy, never once looking up at him. After a few minutes, he cleared his throat.

Machiah: *I'm sorry, Mom. I get these narratives in my head and just run with them. I beat myself up, take how I'm feeling and project it onto you. You care about me more than anyone. You've always been there to give me the real and challenge me to be a better man. I fight against it, and you're right there going toe-to-toe with* *me. I realize that not everyone has a parent willing to give that type of intention… and actually do it. I'm a jerk to you because I'm a jerk to myself. For that, I am sorry. I do want to help out around the house and contribute. I love when you're happy and not stressed out because I did something to make your day smoother. Mom, I'm lazy, and sometimes I don't want to do anything. It sounds horrible, but it's the truth. I'm either on my game and killin' it or flat on my butt destroying myself.*

Mom: *We are our worst critics, Machiah. You're 17 years old. Give yourself some grace. Thank you for manning up. It shows a lot of character and maturity.*

Machiah: *The laundry is finished. It actually gave me some good thinking time. Win-win.*

Everyone has gone through seasons of doubt, self-hatred, and/or self-criticism. Remember to weigh your thoughts. Challenge what you're thinking and saying about God's child. Is it good? Is it profitable? Does it bring you joy or peace? Is it true, or is it just another self-beating? Do the work of processing these destructive thoughts out of your mental space. If left unchecked, it almost always manifests into something that misrepresents your character and the person you're striving to be. Do not be afraid to seek professional care. Sometimes we need a little help climbing out of the pit we dig for ourselves, reframing or seeing things from a fresh perspective. Machiah may be going through typical teenage angst, but we can all remember similar experiences at different milestones in life. Regardless of age or season, it blocks the pathway to a healthy and positive version of yourself. It distorts the communication with loved ones that could otherwise be meaningful and life giving. It also deters us from walking in our purpose and becoming a better version of ourselves.

Transition & Transform

Brandon was a New York state Greco-Roman wrestling champion in 2003. As one of five children living in a small town outside Geneseo, New York, Brandon grew up wrestling with his dad and two brothers. Around the age of seven, he knew he wanted to pursue wrestling full-time. By the age of twelve, his passion for the sport was so fervent that he knew he would go on to wrestle for a college team. Brandon's best buds growing up were physical endurance, brawn, and raw aggression. He wasn't popular in primary school, but the mat instilled confidence, self-assurance, and a stillness about himself. I noticed these qualities the first day I met him. That, and he was physically the picture of athleticism. If you didn't notice his cauliflower ears or broad squared-off shoulders, you would never know there was a beast inside of this quiet 5'9" man. I would later learn that he was incredibly reserved and non-confrontational. Brandon did not engage in verbal or physical altercations unless it called for the beast to come out. At that time in his life, he was either all the way hot or all the way cold. Lukewarmness wasn't in his nature. There is one particular wrestling story that I enjoy hearing him retell. We've been married for nearly ten years. He tells it each time as if it were the first. I love how his eyes light up as he reminisces over his childhood.

One of the biggest wrestling tournaments of the year in Brandon's hometown was the Genesee Valley wrestling tournament. Brandon's father participated in the same event when he was younger. Twenty to twenty-four wrestlers per weight class would compete from all over New York. Brandon had been fighting hard to qualify for this historical event {pineapple!}. The wrestling match that made my husband's face beam with pure joy was the same match that qualified him for the Genesee Valley Wrestling Tournament in 2003. He placed in this tournament at least five times before, but Brandon made a name for himself that year.

It was a semi-final match. A middle-weight class wrestler from South Seneca, New York, stood between

Brandon and another shot at the championship title. For the sake of context, let's call him the bulldog. There were three two-minute rounds to get through. The bulldog won round one straight out of the gates. He quickly demonstrated his superior technique and strength over Brandon. It was a physical chess match. Not only did these athletes need anticipatory and calculated movements, but wrestling also required them to react with absolute certainty of a winning move. Round two. The bulldog took it. Again, Brandon's opponent demonstrated superiority in this round, racking up the points. Round three. Brandon was down five points with fifteen seconds to go. With several switches, reversal, escape, and baited moves, the match was seemingly the bulldog's to take. With five seconds left, Brandon performed a headlock. It contorted the bulldog's entire body, sending him flying in the air, over Brandon's shoulder, and on his back. Brandon used all of his opponent's strength against him in what was a show-worthy moment. He effectively converted the bulldog's energy into a show worthy power move in a fraction of a second. That part of the story makes me think of a dog charging headlong into a cage. Brandon won the match 10 to 12 and gained the title, *The Miracle on the Mat*, subsequently earning him a coveted spot in the Genesee Valley Wrestling Tournament.

Brandon and I have been married for nearly ten years. We have five children. As of January 17, 2022, their ages were 18, 6, 6, 3, and 2. God has truly been a blessing over the years. Hubby did go on to wrestle in college for three years. However, his interest shifted with the realization that wrestling full time could not pay the bills, his student loan debts, or support him financially after graduation. He was a history major. Although wrestling and history were his passions in college, neither would help pay back over $60,000 in tuition loan debt or provide a roof over his head. It was time to retire from wrestling and join the workforce. Brandon's focus went from wrestling to joining the military a year before graduation. His older brother joined the U.S. Navy years prior. Brandon heard about his big brother's overseas deployment tours, beaches, and occupational perks. It sounded like a win-win career move. He dropped everything and joined the Navy in his senior year in 2007. We met as a Hospital Corpsman attached to the 2nd Medical Battalion aboard Camp Lejeune, North Carolina. It was Thursday, January 17, 2013. We spent the entire holiday weekend hanging out, running, swimming, playing Scrabble, and more. We are both super competitive. In retrospect, we naturally had to test each other's metal. I was a pool shark. He whooped my behind in Scrabble. We would race to and from a parking lot near our barracks after each lunch or dinner date. Brandon couldn't get the car in park all the way before I'd jump out to sprint to my barracks room. He'd always catch me just in time to push me out of the way so he could touch the door first! We would fall out laughing every time, stomachs hurting from a half-digested meal. By Sunday afternoon, he asked me to be his girlfriend. Y'all, the man got down on one knee in the middle of a packed restaurant parking lot and asked me to be his girlfriend. It was the longest 60 seconds of my life, but low-key, I was over the moon for it. We were engaged by April 6, 2013, and married three days later. Yes, it was a fast courtship and engagement! Trust me, I know. I found out Brandon was just as impulsive as I was the day I met him. When I have an opportunity to enrich my life, it's difficult to let it go unfulfilled or unaccomplished. When either of us wanted something, we pursued it hard! That certainly was the case the day we met in January. Brandon knew what he wanted when he saw me and locked it down. Machiah turned ten-years-old a few months after we married. Our twin girls were born in 2015. Our third and fourth baby girls followed not long after. I mean, I was pumpin' 'em out. In February 2019, the baby factory closed, and Brandon and I concluded nearly 30 years of combined military service. We were ready to settle down, plant roots, and raise our family. Phew! That was a lot, I know, but the Cliff Notes version gives context to what comes next.

Brandon: *...it was my strategy, babe.*

Me: *So, you were waiting on him to do exactly what you* *wanted him to do?*

Brandon: *I knew he was the superior wrestler. I had to get him to the last part to capitalize on wearing him out.*

Me: *How did you know that if he was the superior wrestler?*

Brandon: *There are certain things your opponent does that are unique. You have to pick up on it, test and verify it, then bait'em.*

Me: *So you knew what move he wanted you in, and you baited him into his go-to move?*

Brandon: *Yes! Exactly. I even made it look like I was struggling.*

Me: *Ohhhh, I see.*

Brandon: *... and babe, it's like anything else in life. If you go so hard but don't pay attention to anything else, it can throw you out of balance. You see, when he'd try to turn into me...*

Me: *... you fed into the turn?*

Brandon: *Yes! I fed into the turn. Initially, I was fighting against it. But just like someone trying to push through a door, he gave a hard shove. Then, PHUMB! I opened the*

door and was on top of him in the same position he had
me in! The look in his eye was like, 'oh, crap.'

There are a lot of similarities between sports and family life. Marriage and family life don't come with a playbook or set rules. Both require time, energy, blood, sweat, and tears. Being married with children can feel like you're constantly making competing choices and wrestling with which direction to take {pineapple!}. If you become fixated on a set routine or go-to moves in a wrestling match, you neglect to see things from the broader perspective that every athlete needs to see in order to make more informed and calculated decisions. A narrow perspective leaves little space to account for the unknown variables your opponent may challenge you with. Likewise, athletes who aren't constantly sharpening their skills and learning new strategies are at a disadvantage. You have to have your head in the fight, on and off the mat. Otherwise, you may find yourself in a compromising position like the bulldog who thought he had Brandon right where he wanted him, only to get flipped on his back, shocked and bewildered. It doesn't matter if you're in the lead, racking up points, or seemingly have your opponent on lockdown. Brandon caught on to the bulldog's system of rudimentary moves and routines. The bulldog's mental fixation on those go-to moves really showed his belly. All Brandon counted on was tiring the bulldog and waited for the right time to strike. We lose critical perspective in the proverbial game when we fixate on tired old routines. I thrive within a certain system and routine but I know it's not enough to sustain a healthy marriage and family life. There is always room to broaden one's perspectives, reframe the lines of thinking, and make positive applications. Success in marriage, raising children, and caring for oneself is about meeting the mental, emotional, and physical challenges. Some fixate on strengthening the body so much that they fail to prepare for those mental and emotional challenges. Others can be so mentally tough yet neglect to train their bodies. A mental challenge requires a level of physical and emotional stamina. A physical fight can feel like playing mental chess. Brandon has seen mentally strong fighters destroy much bigger, yoked-out fighters. Brawn certainly helps, but at the end of the day, the battle belongs to the well-rounded and conditioned fighter.

A person's greatest strength can work against them. We don't necessarily think about our strengths being a downfall, yet we sometimes get thrown onto our backs, thinking we're doing all the right things. After 14 years of successful active-duty service, I concluded active duty life to serve my family full-time at home. I drilled on the weekends with the U.S. Navy Reserves for three years, but it was rough. I was miserable. I loved the Navy, but my head, heart, and hands were committed to my work at home. The love and passion I had for serving my family weren't conducive to what the Navy required of a Chief Petty Officer. I went through a major identity crisis for three years. Work and home life were not symbiotic, and I had no idea why. I am the queen of organization and structure. I'm goal-oriented and always do my best to complete what I put my mind to.

Those skills did not translate well with nursing babies, potty training, teething and whining toddlers, and a hormonal pre-teenage boy. Being a single mother on active duty was a breeze compared to being a full-time mommy at home with (in 2016) three children. During my active-duty days, I'd get home from work and wouldn't take my uniform off until 10pm. Coming home at 4:30-5pm was the start of my second shift. I came home and instantly jumped into cleaning, cooking, helping Machiah with homework, doing my homework, and preparing for the next day. By 10pm, I had a few hours of relaxation to do whatever I wanted before bedtime. As hard as the single mother season was, the days flowed much better than those first few years as a wife and full-time mom at home.

Hubby struggled through some things at home as well. When our twin daughters were born, the hours in the middle of the night were filled with screams, rotating breastfeeding, and diaper changes. Those nights were the gruesome graveyard shifts. Man, it was hard! We both woke up every hour on the hour and then had to be to work by 5:30am for physical training. As a single mother, I was used to having little to no sleep, but it hit differently that year. I almost felt sorry for Hubby. He's built for physically demanding work. Three 12-hour back-to-back shifts with little sleep was nothing compared to twin newborns, a teenager, and maintaining a military career. Juggling family and home life is unique. Being intentionally engaged in family life requires physical, emotional, and mental stamina. The intentionality behind working a full-time job, keeping house, raising children, cultivating a marriage, and being the best version of yourself can take a lot out of a person. Finding the time and mustering the energy to have fun in between all of that is an added chore. Hubby was not prepared for the mental and emotional challenge. The physical demands of my day nearly wrecked me. Whether you're a stay-at-home parent or full-time in the workforce, it doesn't matter. Family life is hard work! During my first year as a stay-at-home mommy, I questioned how I could be a rock star all day for the Navy but struggled at home. How could I be home all day long yet still struggle to maintain a sense of order? What was the disconnect between rocking it in one area of life and completely bombing it in another?

The answer lies in how intentional and consistent we are. Learning how to transition from rocking in one area to functioning just as well in other areas is an evolutionary process. When we become proficient in one thing, we tend to fall into an unconscious state of complacency. Like we've arrived. No need to go further. In the words of Thanos, "The work will always be done." On the contrary, because we are not perfect beings, there will always be space for continued growth. Ideally, we should be of the mindset to move and grow continuously, sharpening and challenging ourselves. It doesn't have to be fast. It doesn't have to create unnecessary stress or anxiety. It should, however, be consistent. We should all have a healthy hunger to broaden and adjust our perspectives and skill sets as the seasons of life change. Brandon and I were mentally, physically, and emotionally capable of overcoming some tough challenges in life. Brandon spent his entire formative years proving to be self-aware and able to make sound decisions. In wrestling, he had to be conscious of his surroundings, time his movements wisely, and be a quick learner. These were a culmination of natural talents and acquired skills. These were abilities that won awards, accolades, and titles.

There are critically important questions anyone with such strengths and skills should ask themselves when transitioning from adolescence to single adulthood, marriage, and parenthood. Do our skills and abilities cease to exist because we are no longer on the proverbial mat? Have we been blessed with skills and abilities that are exclusively useful in one area or season? Are they meant for a singular purpose, or can they be as powerful if utilized in other areas of life? Here's what I've learned in answering those questions; if your heart isn't in the task in front of you, transforming those skills to be useful in all areas of your life will likely never happen. If harnessed and channeled, we can take the same passions and talents unique to us and discover ways to apply them to situations we wouldn't think would be useful. This is especially true for areas where we struggle the most. For example, I spent 17 years of my life serving my country. I advanced to the rank of a Chief Petty Officer, all while raising a son alone for the first ten years and growing my family for the remaining seven years. I've been deployed to Iraq and have been in numerous leadership roles worldwide. I was living the best version of myself during my military days. When I married the love of my life, active duty life was no longer conducive to having the family dynamic I desired. I chose family and retired from the military lifestyle.

Separating from the Navy felt like a divorce. I went through a major identity crisis. Physically, I transitioned from having the body and stamina of a 20-something-year-old athlete to... well, you can imagine how multiple pregnancies wear on the body. Psychologically and emotionally, I didn't give myself much time to transition into civilian life, being a full-time mom at home and an educator. I wanted to take all my natural talents and the abilities I'd gleaned from my military days and pour them into raising a family. After all, being at home all day would be my new normal. A few short years into my new normal, I discovered that it was undoubtedly one of the most challenging transitions I'd ever experienced. But that was exactly what it was: a transition. I wasn't acquainted with the new woman in the new season of my life. I was completely free to make my own choices, yet I had never felt so defeated, broken, insecure, and lost. I didn't feel worthy of anything special in my marriage. I felt overwhelmingly used and worn out as a mother. Most days, I functioned as if I were the live-in nanny. My life consisted of a routine that lacked fun, excitement, and passion. I was going along with the routines of life. Completely devoid of imagination or a desire to branch out and explore what I was capable of in this new season of life. With that type of rudimentary mindset, I thought I had become the least capable woman on the planet.

How far, I was convinced, I'd fallen. Homelife was stable, but I certainly wasn't happy nor close to thriving alone at home most days. The problem wasn't that I was ill prepared for the challenges of stay-at-home life. The problem was that I was not taking care of myself physically and mentally. I was barely hanging on to my sanity. That was how overwhelmed and burnt out I was. I no longer enjoyed working at home. Instead, I started to resent my choice to stay home full-time. I'd lost passion and purpose in the work of my hands. It led to days when I didn't want to do life anymore. I did not want to cause bodily harm to myself. I simply did not want to be in this life. I'd lost perspective and purpose in the tunnel vision of the routine I found myself in. I treated home and family life like a regimented military lifestyle. It just did not translate the same.

Slowly and with professional help, I discovered what worked best for me. I learned how to take all my natural abilities and acquired skills to create a sustainable home life where I could thrive as an individual and have fun in the day-to-day grind. Hubby and I also discovered a lot about our marriage and partnership. We made radical adjustments to how we functioned as a team. An old pastor of mine called this the sweet spot. It's the space where you know you fit in and things are functioning as intended. You and your environment have a sense of stability, even in a storm or times of uncertainty. By God's grace, I transitioned from being burnt out and hopeless into having an empowered and capable mindset. I discovered how to transition all the passion and success that carried me through my military tenure into an incredibly healthy and functional home life. The actual transformation was in the application. I made concerted efforts to prioritize my mental and physical health. Reserving time to care for my mental and physical health became medicine. Each time I went for a run, retreated to my room to pray and meditate, or scheduled an outing with a friend, it was medical treatment for me. The evidence that I was gaining traction in my whole health treatment plan was when I achieved greater mental clarity and had more energy.

Having energy and mental clarity gave me the space and motivation to create outlets in which I could express my passions, rediscover my purpose, and find some much-needed joy. Writing was one of those outlets. I had years worth of journal entries, audio recordings, and other content. Consolidating and formatting my writings into books and creating products based on my experiences at home came naturally. It was the perfect outlet to share my thoughts and frustrations in a positive and productive way. Again, the heart has to be in it. Transitioning into the mother, father, or parent we are called to be requires head and heart. To be able to navigate through the grinding years well takes intentionality and consistent engagement. Our bodies will fail us. We will get beat down most days. Like me, you may start things off on the wrong foot. The life or *fill-in-the-blank* that you envision for yourself may not come easily. Most things in life take serious work and commitment. If other commitments in life overrule family priorities, we cannot expect to see the vision for the family come to fruition. Good news: God says His grace is sufficient for the day. I take that verse of scripture l-i-t-e-r-a-l-l-y. He didn't say tomorrow or yesterday. It means today, I HAVE everything I need to face the challenges of the day. It's up to me to recognize that provision and use what God has already provided. There is always a choice to do better, to be better. The years ahead can be remarkably better than the years behind.

Ego and pride must be addressed when discussing effective transition and transformation because it involves change. Change isn't always a welcoming feeling or concept. We naturally fight against change for one reason or another. When discussing the transitioning of skills from one area of life to another, a change must occur. My transition from being a single mother in the military to being married with multiple children at home required change. For Brandon to be an effective husband and father, changes had to be made as our family grew. Even now, as I approach the age of 40, change is expected if I want to mature into a better

107

version of myself. Many people will go to extreme lengths to ensure they are viewed a certain way, no matter what season they're in. Care is placed more on how we are viewed by others rather than how we view ourselves. How we desire to see ourselves, rather than facing who we really are when we look in the mirror, is a powerful deterrent. It's an image that creates an alter ego within us. After so many years of building an image and feeding the ego, we become what we create, making it that much more difficult to recognize the person in the mirror. Image. Hmmm. We build images for ourselves. This reminds me of how God warns against making idols and worshiping them. Sure, we're not creating physical statues that we bow down to and worship, but we do build images for ourselves then submit our hearts and energy to maintaining them. Have you ever thought about your ego in terms of idolatry? Creating a self-made image for the approval and praise of others is common in our society. We crave a certain level of attention and recognition. It feeds the ego. From my observation, pride and insecurities are usually associated with a big ego. People will protect their pride, image and source of social validation to no end. When left unchecked, it can wreck a person. There is no room for ego and pride in healthy relationships. First things first, strip that ego!

I would like you to seriously consider how you mentally, spiritually, and emotionally prepare for conflict or maintain the chaos in your life. When you want to have words with your spouse or need to have it out with a coworker, what do you do in the moments leading up to the confrontation? Because I carry my stress in my spine and stomach, I usually need to pray, go for a run, or do something physical to clear my mind. The times when I was dealing with a ridiculously unreasonable coworker, I had to give myself extra love to keep from festering over how people could be so unreasonable. When I was in the workforce, I'd get off from work some days and go directly to the store to buy myself flowers. To this day, I still enjoy arranging flowers in pretty vases and placing them around the house to soothe my spirit. I play worship or soft cafè music as background noise in my home to keep my thoughts from wandering in an unproductive direction. If a conversation with a friend or loved one goes south, it's refreshing to wake up to the smell of flowers and the ambiance of beauty and calmness. Whatever you do to prepare for confrontation or maintain the chaos in your life, clear your mind and get ready to dig deep. This is where conflict may be required to make those healthy changes. Let's go to work.

Grab some paper or a notebook and a pen. On one side of the paper, list your unique skills, talents, special abilities, and gifts. Relate them to a time when you knew you were the best version of yourself and thrived. Sit in those memories for a moment. Smile and reminisce. On the other side of the paper, write those areas in your work, home, or personal life where you are struggling, fumbling, failing, and all-around suck. I've heard people say that they were sucking at life. Write it down and be specific. Take notice of the gap between your most amazing self and the areas where you are not so amazing. Analyze the gap. What was happening in your life before, during, and after that gap of time? Are there notable physical or mental variances? If you have a bunch of physical gifts on one side of the paper and a bunch of emotionally and mentally challenging areas that you wrestle with on the other side, think of how these two sides of the paper can merge. Ask yourself, how can I take all the things I'm great at and apply them to the areas where I'm not so great? Be extremely realistic. This is not the time to daydream or lie to yourself. It will only lead you back to that false image we so easily create for ourselves. If change was easy, you would have implemented it a long time ago. It isn't that simple, and the benefits of being honest with yourself are far more rewarding in the long run.

Here is a healthy gauge to see if you're being honest with yourself. Does it hurt when you discover a character flaw, a pattern of poor choices, unwholesome friendships, or an appropriate action you've been avoiding? Does healthy change require acknowledging a monster inside of you? Will change require exposing truths that will discredit you or possibly destroy a relationship you're desperately trying to maintain? As painful as it will be, that is probably the direction you should be progressing towards to make positive and sustainable change. The most painful decisions we have to make are the ones that cause us to give up something, be exposed, or knock us off a pedestal. Brandon and I went through some tough changes over the years. In 2020, we put it all on the table and completely transformed our marriage. We discovered the power in being vulnerable and painfully honest. If it's difficult for you to be vulnerable with yourself, invite a trusted friend or loved one to join the discussion. Someone who knows you well and isn't afraid to tell it how it is. Don't get defensive or angry at the messenger! That is the quickest way to burn bridges and lose a trusted friend. Afterall, how many people do you have in your life that are willing to give it to you straight? If you don't like what they have to say, simply say *thank you* and at least chew on the facts instead of responding out of hurt feelings. The process of change isn't supposed to feel good. It usually hurts. Do you know what hurts worse? Telling someone you love and respect the truth to their face and getting your head bit off for it. Owch! The people who speak truth into your life love and respect you. Read Proverbs 27:6. It was a painful lesson for me once I understood I was throwing my pearls to dogs and swine. Read Matthew 7:6. Having honest discussions is designed to uproot whatever is stunting your growth or blocking positive change. It most likely isn't what you want to hear, so prepare your spirit and heart. Hubby and I decided to fill each other's gap. We switched papers, read each other's strengths and weaknesses, and wrote recommendations on closing the gap. We agreed that no matter what we discover about ourselves or the other person, we will face it head-on. We both knew our strengths and capabilities since the day we met. Now we had to identify the cause of those gaps and the areas where we struggled in our home and family life. Hubby's passivity was hurting him as a husband and father. My overbearing demeanor blinded me. He craved more sex. I was starving for intimacy. He felt he had no space to make decisions without me shooting down everything that came out of his mouth. I perceived him as a benefactor who contributed the minimum. You get the picture. Vulnerable and honest.

The real work can begin once the cause of gaps is identified and necessary changes are established. This will look different for each person, marriage, relationship, and family dynamic. It will also require time to notice the tangible effects of change. Hubby and I had to cut out, repurpose, cultivate, and transition a lot over the space of a year. Neither of us got everything we wanted as individuals, but our marriage and family dynamic got what it needed to thrive. A happy home life was worth the adjustments I had to make. Hubby discovered all the rewards for his hard work, intentionality, and consistency. We both created space to live and function as our authentic selves and had energy left over for each other. That's the best part and what our 'sweet spot' looks like. Our intimacy and connectedness as a team grow stronger as we improve as individuals. Every day, I am grateful to have a man who loves and adores me enough to do the work with me. I feel like Shug Avery from *The Color Purple*. That man would drink my dirty bathwater y'all! That's how much Brandon Thomas Clark loves me. Hubby would say I love him more than he loves himself. It is nearly obsessive how I constantly strive to improve our home life and ensure every family member feels invested in, loved, and cared for. Hubby would take on a gang in Portland, Oregon if another man said something slick to me. True story, by the way. He would die for our children and me without hesitating. I feel completely safe with him. Brandon knows I will go to war for him. Friends, mother, father, sister, brother, cousin...it doesn't matter. Do not disrespect my man. Brandon is extremely romantic and always looks for opportunities to make a black girl blush. Every so often, we have to go back to the drawing board and close an unattended gap, but for the most part, we're happy to be in a space where major realignments aren't needed.

So! Time's up! No more facade. No more pretending.

Be vulnerable. Call out those insecurities and put them in writing. Find the solution. Figure out how to transition and transform those strengths. Don't think the work is done just because you found a solution to the struggles in your life, relationship, work, or family dynamic. Remember, there is always space for growth and improvement. Be consistent. It can be terrifying to expose yourself when all you want to do is retreat into your own happy shell of mediocracy. Hubby and I have found great freedom in our transition and transformation processes. We are by no stretch of the imagination perfect. We still get on each other's nerves. We occasionally let each other down. The difference is in how quickly we recover from those inevitable letdowns. We no longer linger on our shortcomings and failures. We have created contingencies for ourselves. Contingencies to maintain the checks and balances. We work to keep the gaps bridged, keep our perspectives open and adjust when necessary. Best of all, we wake up knowing we are living the best versions of ourselves.

Insecurities & Projecting

One of my husband's classmates in college was a first-generation Afghan American. Her parents spent ten years in a refugee camp before resettling in the states. For the sake of context, we'll call her Aaliyah. Aaliyah was the first in her family to attend college. She was a pre-med major. It was the first day of the fall semester. She and Brandon took part in a class team-building exercise. A sort of *icebreaker* experience for all the new students. They were tasked with completing an assignment and afterward talk amongst themselves to get to know each other better. Here is how their *icebreaker* went after completing the assignment:

Brandon: *Hey guys, great job. We did good work. BOOM!!* (hand gestures an explosion).
Aaliyah: *Oh, I see.*
Brandon: *What's that?*
Aaliyah: *Because I'm Afghan, I'm automatically a*

117

terrorist.

Brandon: *What? Why would you say that?*

Aaliyah: *It's pretty obvious who the racist is in the group.*

None of the other group members said a word. Brandon did not know how to respond and was flabbergasted by the entire exchange. Aaliyah sat back in her seat as if she had just sucker punched Brandon. Needless to say, this was an extremely awkward and confusing icebreaker. It's also a painful example of *projecting,* according to Sigmund Freud. From my experience, negative *projecting* is when a person takes unresolved conflict within themselves and dumps it on another person. It often takes the form of passive-aggressive speech and behavior and is most likely subconscious. In other circumstances, it's flat-out evident. Someone says or does something clearly to cause harm. The unresolved internal conflict has built up, and they want you to hurt just as badly as they do. The attacks that come from a psychological or emotional position are the worst. They are hard to call out and easy to deny.

Situations like what happened to Brandon make me think of the law of conservation of energy. Energy cannot be created or destroyed. It can only be transferred. I think of the body as a vessel that takes in, stores, and releases energy daily. Some store more positive energy than negative, and vice versa. They may make a concerted effort to have a pleasant attitude, exercise regularly, eat a clean diet, maintain healthy friendships, and similar intentional lifestyle choices. Others, unfortunately, hold on to negative energy, like Gollum from the *Lord of the Rings*. Negative energy manifests in the body as stress, physical pain, toxic behavior, or speech; these examples are not exhaustive. After listening to what happened to Brandon in class and reflecting on similar situations in my own life, I wanted to understand the nature of energy more. Specifically, how to identify when negative energy is projected at me and understand the power I possess to change its effect on my body.

It is said the best medicine is preventive medicine. I

avoid negative energy like the Coronavirus. There should be masks to prevent someone's lousy attitude from getting into my system. As I get older, I view the projection of negative energy on me as a direct assault on my health. After a rude encounter with the gremlin at the license and title office, I found myself whipping my shirt and arms like a puddle of mud was splattered on me. Yuck! Stress is a slow killer. I'm not a doctor, but I've lived long enough to understand how it wreaks havoc on the body. I've also lived long enough to recognize when someone is maliciously projecting their garbage onto me. It could be for sport, out of complete ignorance, or perhaps boredom. Projecting may also be a cry for help despite its ugly delivery. Regardless, I do not believe the body was designed to be a vessel for toxic stress and other harmful garbage. It is everyone's responsibility to sort through, name, manage, and/or dispose of their own internal garbage. And here we are again. It takes intentionality and consistency.

God wired my mind and emotions to see and feel the pains of others. This is especially true as it pertains to projecting. I'm sensitive to the energy of others. When someone comes at me with passive aggression or a straight-up disrespectful attitude, the majority of the time, I'm able to manage or diffuse the situation fairly quickly. It could be a simple misunderstanding in communication. Everyone deserves the benefit of the doubt. Perhaps they are having a bad day and haven't had the chance to decompress. Maybe they are working through something, and I caught them on an off day. Some people are just equal-opportunity jerks. There have been times when a situation had nothing to do with projecting, just some jerk who clearly needed to be called out and checked. I have no problem doing so as directly and respectfully as humanly possible. My default is to diffuse the situation amicably. I've also learned to let a lot of crap go. Most of the time, it isn't worth the energy {pineapple!}. If I let the projections of people stress, upset and overwhelm me, I'll have a physical reaction. It starts with irritability in my spirit and a minor stomachache. When under attack by a large amount of negative energy, my spine aches, my head hurts, and I have a burning sensation in my stomach. The pain will put me in the fetal position. The amount of self-control it takes to combat what often feels like an army of broken, hurting, and angry people can wear on the body and spirit. Here is where grace comes in. I understand the fragility of life, how broken people are, and how everyone is going through something. I remind myself that God has already provided me with what I need to get through the day. It's up to me to take what has been provided and use it.

When someone projects their internal turmoil onto another, it can be hard to identify or understand what's happening. The shock and confusion can take a minute to process. Naturally, an off-guard reply is needed to calm down the tension. "It's all good." "Not a problem." "Don't worry about it." I enjoy watching the wittier personalities dish out on cue and clever responses. It's like they're walking around, locked and loaded, ready to fire off insult for insult. Being on the defense, waiting, and expecting someone to attack with negative energy can be exhausting. I don't believe the body is meant to go through life in that type of defense posture. Negative projecting doesn't always take the form of a nasty attitude. It can also take the form of being overly polite and accommodating, very much like passive aggression. Have you ever looked into someone's eyes as they smiled and agreed with you? Their eyes look frustrated, worried, in pain, or even angry. The eyes don't lie and will always tell on the soul. Negative projecting will actively try to mischaracterize, discourage, belittle, demean, or do emotional harm. Has anyone ever called you a loser? Said that you lacked an ability or character trait to accomplish something you've been dreaming of for years? Or, more subtly, discourage you from taking a risk or making a change to better yourself? More often than not, that's how they feel about themselves. You are the innocent bystander on the receiving end of their unresolved garbage.

A good friend of mine shared a conversation with me about an exchange with a friend she worked with. For the sake of privacy, let's call them Amber and Jackie. Lovely names. On the surface, the conversation should have been casual, lighthearted, and harmless. My friend Amber had just reached a milestone in her diet and fitness goals. She was so proud of herself and thrilled to share it with Jackie. Jackie clearly didn't share in her enthusiasm.

Amber: *Yaaaaaass, hoonnneyyy! It's my weigh day, and I am so proud of myself. I dropped seven pounds since my last weigh day. I'm gaining traction with this weight loss plan.*

Jackie: *Yea, but don't get too excited. A lot of people lose weight at first, only to gain it all back again, plus more.*

Amber: *Well, it's working for me, boo-boo, and I'm already seeing the results. Look at this booty and them hips, though. I'm getting my apple bottom back! I'm definitely going to celebrate this small victory.*

Jackie: *IF you stay on track. You're technically still in the beginning phases, so calm down, girl. Don't get too excited. It's probably water weight and poop. After two months of eating like a rabbit (as she chuckles to herself), let's see how you do.*

Amber: *Thanks for reminding me. The plan guidelines say it'll be easier if I focus on the small goals in front of me and give myself kudos for every effort made. It'll drive me crazy if I think about how many more months I have to "eat like a rabbit" so chill, I got this.*

Jackie: *You have to meal prep for two weeks at a time, so you kinda have to think about all those months you're gonna be eating the same thing over and over.*

Amber: *Yeeeeah, I know, but I'll be ok. I know where my focus should be. I got this.*

Jackie: *How much research did you do on your so-called plan? It really sounds like one of those gimmicky weight loss plans. I don't think it's healthy for you. You need carbs for energy and meat for protein. I hope you're not wasting your time only to get bored and quit.*

Yuck! Do you feel the negativity and passive aggression dripping off the page? Ugh! It hurt my spine listening to that story. Amber was repeatedly trying to reaffirm her commitment to her weight loss goals. Whether she knew it or not, she was actively trying to feed her mind and body positive energy to combat the obvious challenges associated with weight loss. Jackie might as well have told Amber she had zero faith in her and that Amber would be miserable with her body for the rest of her life. It's almost as though Jackie's hostile posture was actively trying to strip Amber of anything that could positively affirm her. They really were not having the same conversation. For Jackie, it was a tit-for-tat toxic ping-pong game. She was actually playing ping pong against a wall in her mind. All Amber did was invite Jackie to share her joy and excitement. What a mistake that was. I've been there! My heart goes out to all the Jackies of the world. I'm sure she cares about her friend, but the negativity Jackie projected onto Amber was most likely related to something she was struggling with internally. Instead of dumping (however subconscious it may be) all that built-up negativity onto Amber, Jackie could take the time to explore how she views her own body or the goals she sets for herself. Perhaps she's failing at something, fearful of taking risks or making transformations in her own life. Whatever the reason, seeing Amber's happiness and success triggered something in Jackie, who, in turn, chose not to be a supportive friend. We must take a step back, examine ourselves, and put a name to the toxic garbage that eats away at us. In this scenario, jealousy and envy are some of the worst toxic energies that can spoil a relationship. Putting a name to the mess inside us gives us a target to begin sorting, managing, and/or disposing of the garbage within.

Similar to Brandon and Aaliyah's exchange, projecting can almost always be identified within the first few moments of meeting someone, in a tense verbal exchange, or straight up randomly and out of nowhere. Keyword, *tension*. Tension has a way of marinating inside us and seeping into innocent bystanders. There were times when I felt like I was in a decent mood when suddenly, I was triggered by someone's facial expression or tone of voice, and SNAP! Verbal vomit explodes out of my mouth. I can see the monster coming up and out of my throat in those moments. I'm just as shocked as the poor victim of my projected anger and frustration. I usually try to apologize, have a conversation, or make amends. When I have some quiet time, I always carefully examine what possessed me and why. Otherwise, it's stored inside of me, unresolved. That's where it starts. The random outburst of emotions is how my garbage tells on me. Most of my insecurities take me back to middle and high school, where I had to endure being called racially degrading names regularly. I remember the hateful facial expressions of girls my age who would take turns greeting the only brown girl in class with a new spin on the same derogatory names. It was as if they had regular morning meetings to discuss new and creative ways to dig at me. The first boy to ever ask me to be his girlfriend was Caucasian. His name was Matthew. We were in seventh grade. I always thought he was cute, but understandably assumed he would never be interested in me. Afterall, it was Asheville, North Carolina in the early 1990s. One day, and out of the blue, he asked me to be his girlfriend. It was the very first time we'd ever spoken to one another. I was shocked that he even knew my name. Besides his beautiful blue eyes, gentle smile, and friendly disposition, I knew nothing else about him. I giddily said yes and had to book it to class. You should have seen me in English class that day. I was over the moon, happy, shocked, nervous, and excited that a boy was interested in me for the first time in my life. Me. The awkward, nerdy brown girl that got called disgusting names up and down the hallways. By the end of English class that day, Matthew walked over to me for the second and final time. He dumped me. His facial expression clearly communicated embarrassment, social pressure, and confusion. The poor boy didn't know that it wasn't cool to date a brown girl and that his social status would be jeopardized if people found out. Guess he didn't read the memo on the KKK announcement board that morning. Perhaps it was the first time he experienced racism and social pressure. Whatever the reason, he was not down to join me in that torment. What young boy would want to stand with me as a handful of our fellow 7th graders stared, laughed, and shook their heads in disgust every day?

Best believe the torment followed me through high school. To this day, I still cringe when walking in public spaces and randomly catch someone giving me what I perceive as a gruesome look of disgust. Some people cannot control their facial expressions. It's like they spent the last 15 years of their life frowning, and now their face is stuck like that. It is puzzling how people aren't aware that they are walking around with a facial expression that looks like they have dog poop on their upper lip. Those are the same faces I have to look at in the Target self-check-out line. Staring, as if they're trying to figure me out. Whatever it is that put a permanent look of hate on their face, it triggers my insecurities, and I relive the trauma from grade school. Is there something about my appearance or presence that is undesirable or offensive? Is this person a racist who wishes I would drop dead? Are they trying to figure out why my curls stand up the way they do? Do I stank? I manage my insecurities with the truth of who

God says I am. God's truth of how I was created, uniquely wired, and made for a specific purpose are thoughts I replay in my mind throughout my day. I combat feelings with facts. The fact is, I am fearfully and wonderfully made. It is a fact that I am beautiful, intelligent, bold, charismatic, a little weird, occasionally scatterbrained, sensitive, courageous, and pleasantly surprising. When I encounter some poopy-lip person giving me the stank eye, my insecurities may trigger, but truth overwhelms my spirit and puts me at ease. I choose to project a warm smile and continue on with my day.

Feelings are incredibly transitory. They come and go as quickly as our insecurities are triggered. Objective truth is undisturbed, reliable, and gives a tremendous sense of security. When a person is aware of their insecurities and is doing the work to manage them, there is a genuineness in their engagement with other people. It's truly a refreshing experience. I say 'manage' insecurities because some never really go away if we're honest. If anything, we often trade one insecurity for another, depending on the season we're going through. Regardless, we can learn to manage our responses when those insecurities are triggered. When people and places spark an uncomfortable memory from my childhood, the involuntary emotional response is almost palpable. It can be painful and tempting to lash out.

I've noticed that men and women who are secure in themselves have genuine care toward the welfare of others. It's organic, and they tend to blend in with the people around them, no matter the demographic. They don't stiffen up or appear unsettled in social encounters. There isn't an immediate sense of competition or disapproval around an alpha personality. There certainly isn't a combative or aggressive spirit about their countenance. On the contrary, there is a refreshing air about a secure woman desiring to engage with people she understands might also be facing the same fight as she does every day. The warmth she projects shouts with a desire to genuinely know a person's heart, no matter how brief the encounter is. Similarly, a man who is secure in his insecurities owns it! He isn't afraid to hold it on display for the world to see. He doesn't hide his insecurities behind a shell of a man. He's not afraid of exposing pain, failure, or being labeled as less than a man. There isn't anyone on the planet who hasn't dealt with pain, shame, failure, or inadequacies. I believe a real man wears his flaws like a man because, quite literally, they are only flaws. They have no power. If an imperfection, inadequacy, or failure has that much power to completely change the definition of what it means to embody manhood, what would be the point of striving to be a better man? Your insecurities have already won the war and are holding you down by the freakin' neck. There is no space for growth, maturity, or striving for greatness if a man or woman relinquishes his/her God given power with a single word, insecurity. As a result, we project our powerless posture onto others.

Hubby made a great point about how some men fight against change when it's perceived negatively. He would tell anyone today how his pride got in the way of positive change in the early years of our marriage. He perceived my suggestions as "needles of corrections." Correction equaled disrespect in his mind. Case in point, when Hubby and I were in what Priscilla Shirer calls "heated fellowship" (I love you, Priscilla!), I often felt he didn't care about addressing weak spots in our marriage. Brandon was under the impression that I was trying to change the core of who he was versus simply addressing a character concern. Some of our discussions would go back and forth for months unresolved. Nothing changed. Keyword: *change*. Marinate on that word for a moment. Change is a natural evolutionary process. It's less about changing your spouse's personality, what they're passionate about, or personal constitution. On the contrary, a natural evolution must take place for an individual and a relationship to mature. If the relationship isn't growing, what exactly is happening? A spouse's attempt to *change*, aka grow, the relationship can appear controlling. For Hubby and I, my asking to go to marital counseling to work on the marriage, learn to communicate more effectively, and figure out how to function as a team more intentionally was all about change. For Hubby, it was undesirable and unwelcomed. Today, he calls me his "adversarial helper," with the understanding that without tension, growth can't occur. If we're not changing, aka *evolving*, as individuals, wives, husbands, parents, lovers, and friends, what exactly are we doing day after day, year after year? Doesn't the process of maturing into the best version of ourselves involve change? If so, change is something we should look forward to and welcome.

Projecting and the transference of energy were referenced earlier in this chapter. In the Clark Family Homeschool, teaching children emotional and spiritual intelligence is just as important as arithmetic and the sciences. In a world full of energy exchanges, understanding the spiritual and emotional part of our being is vitally important in our children's development. Learning how to recognize, process, and repurpose the energy that people store and release daily is vital to responding well to the negative and positive projections of others. My husband has blonde hair, blue eyes, and an athletic build. I jokingly tell him he has an American apple pie face and blue eyes filled with sunshine and rainbows. An initial encounter with Brandon Thomas Clark certainly screams 'American Made.' Aaliyah felt comfortable enough to voice her underhanded and prejudiced remarks at Brandon in front of a group of their peers. Her icebreaker moment put Brandon in a tense and uncomfortable position, labeled him a racist, and created a disturbing awkwardness in the group before anyone could remember each other's names. Upon meeting Brandon for the first time, from Aaliyah's perspective, he fell into one category purely based on his physical features: a blond-haired, blue-eyed, white racist. Before Brandon could even speak on his behalf, some unresolved garbage dwelling in Aaliyah's spirit was clearly triggered. Brandon was the innocent bystander on whom all that unresolved garbage was dumped.

God spoke the world into existence. He...spoke.

When He created mankind, He said it was very good. God said it. Yet, men can 'think' he is inadequate and live an entire lifetime in that powerlessness. God fashioned Eve, yet women can live a lifetime thinking they're ordinary and can't see anything beautiful or unique about themselves. If the God of the Universe created you out of his own image and distinguished you as unique above everything else in creation, who are we to believe anything less? As fragile and powerless as we posture ourselves in our insecurities, how can we pick apart our identity and live as if what's left over is absolutely true? A man is secure when he's aware of his imperfections and still carries himself as the man God created him to be. The stillness of a man grounded in the trueness of his identity is rare, refreshing, and comforting. It intrigues people rather than propels them away with toxic feelings of fear and intimidation. I knew a great man like that once. He had firm confidence, yet he was the gentlest person you'd ever meet. He embodied true manhood and was a model of meek masculinity. He was strong when he needed to be.

Courageous when the situation called for it. Gentle when it mattered and unapologetically stood alone when the majority didn't agree with him. He spoke about his vulnerabilities with complete strangers, anyone who needed to hear or was willing to listen. He was self-taught in a lot of things. He matured spiritually and emotionally to be sensitive to what people were really saying when they projected their pain onto him. He listened to their heart cries and knew how to respond in love, desperately searching for the truth to comfort them. This man was my twin brother, Carlyle Jameson Miller. Often, men hide behind the excuse that they were not taught how to be a man, a father, or a husband. It was not modeled or taught in the home growing up, giving them more of a license to act recklessly and lack intentionality in their adult life. They came from environments that stifled their maturity as capable and strong men. That's what a lot of adult males tell their wives and children. I have this crazy idea that none of us got exactly what we needed to be successful in life, marriage, and family. Your earthly father didn't have to formally teach you to be a man. Your earthly mother didn't have to be there to nurture you into womanhood. We fail each other miserably, but it doesn't matter because God created you and said it is very good. The culture will pressure and marginalize you, but you're still a man. Society will label and stereotype you because you share the same race or bodily features as someone else. It does not matter. You're a child of the King. Jesus wasn't some macho figure, but he could still tear up a temple if what was going on inside wasn't right. He wasn't loud or boisterous but could put another man in his place for speaking recklessly about His Father's creation. He was in darkness and alone often, despised, rejected, scoffed at, betrayed, and minimized. However, he was still fully man and fully God and carried Himself as such consistently. Even when He was hanging on a cross, seemingly powerless, He did not stop functioning in His purpose. Society often impresses on people in ways that create distortion and division. We all project something. It would be foolish to think only happy, bubbly people project goodness and sunshine while the Eeyores of the world are just sad sacks of despair and misery. Try to reframe projecting from a utilitarian point of view. If we understand the nature of fire, we learn how to harness and use it to our benefit. Having and maintaining a healthy perspective is essential when navigating self-identity and value, creating and maintaining healthy relationships, and discovering how to best respond to emotional triggers.

Proverbs 25:2 says that it is the glory of God to conceal a matter, but it is the honor of kings to search out a matter. All the answers to our questions have already been answered. It's our job to take the time to seek out those answers. Finding the answers to the struggle doesn't always promise a solution. Sometimes, the imperfections we learn about ourselves are meant to keep us humble. Jacob lived with a bad hip. A body image insecurity may remind you to be intentional in taking care of your vessel. Identity insecurity may remind you to look to God to reaffirm who you are in Him. That destructive self-talk we try to suppress so badly could be the very thing that makes you the perfect candidate to be a big brother, a Miss Clara from *War Room*, or a mentor for the next generation. Name those insecurities. Be honest with yourself, no matter how painful the process is. You can still find the courage to face those demons that keep you broken and bitter. Reframe your thinking. Create realistic and tangible ways to not only manage how you project onto others but also create original ways to thrive in the vessel that the Master Potter has molded you into, imperfections and all.

Self-Love & Boundaries

Have you ever reached a point in life where the walls felt like they were closing in? The weight of work life becomes so unbearable you have anxiety on Sunday morning, dreading going to work on Monday. The most challenging parts of your weekday morning routine are waking up to get the kids on the bus by 7:00am, packing lunches, and putting on something decent for the day. Right after the July 4th holiday, Christmas trees are already stocked in retail stores everywhere. Can we end the summer and enjoy the fall season before thinking about the end of the year?! For those who were not so blessed to have amazing in-laws, you'll have to start thinking of an excuse to get out of the annual Thanksgiving get-together. I personally dread Christmas shopping for coworkers, friends and family I barely know or even talk to. It's weird and awkward! There are seasons in a marriage that seem to cripple the spirit due to years of dysfunction, ineffective communication, a lack of partnership, and/or poor choices. I could name several circumstances in my own life that broke me mentally and physically. Seasons where I felt like I'd be the youngest woman on the planet to have a heart attack. The first five years of my marriage were the most confusing times of my life. Hubby made me want to scratch my eyeballs out. I'm sure I'm the reason for the gray in his beard. When and how do we draw a line in the sand? For me, it was after the second visit to the ER and being prescribed medication for panic attacks and uncontrolled vomiting. My body was screaming for help and a change, but I didn't know how to restore the peace without wrecking relationships or pooping where I slept. We have to work to earn a living. The environment in which we live and people at work aren't promised to be pleasant or stable. It's not like you can pick the fun in-laws to spend Christmas with and vanquish the rude and disrespectful sister-in-law. Marriages evolve as the seasons come and go. Working towards that version of utopia for your life and relationship takes time, energy, and patience.

In March 2020, I broke. I lost myself under the weight of being everything to everyone. I was exhausted being a wife, mom, daughter/sister-in-law, chef, housekeeper, chauffeur, schoolteacher, peacemaker, therapist, accountant, nurse, scheduler, cheerleader, disciplinarian, party planner, negotiator, and the list goes on. I left no space for the person who needed my attention the most. It was like sprinting in place every day, going nowhere. The only thing that was moving forward was time. I no longer saw the point of life. It didn't make sense how I was investing so much time and energy into raising my family and maintaining relationships yet feeling completely empty and purposeless. Likewise, it made no sense how I had so much to be grateful for, yet I no longer wanted to be in this life. I knew I needed an intervention, and fast. For the first time in my life, I was afraid of myself and how I reasoned through thoughts of not wanting to be alive. The grass was looking greener on the other side with every meaningless human interaction. The straw that broke the camel's back was a typical weekday morning in the kitchen. I honestly couldn't say what brought on that particular panic attack. All I knew was that I saw red, my head was throbbing in pain, my heart was beating out of my chest, and the Cutco knife on the counter looked like an opportunity to end it all. Hubby looked at me with confusion and pain in his eyes that day. It broke my heart not to be able to explain what was going on with me and how he could help. He didn't know what to do or say. I grabbed the car keys and walked out the door. Hubby had no idea where I was going or when I'd be back. I drove to the nearest Veteran Affairs Medical Center and checked myself into the mental health clinic.

Giving of yourself as a mother and wife can be draining. Investing in a family is a true labor of love. There is no immediate gratification, and the return on investment can take years to see. It took over a year of healing and therapy to get back on a forward progressing track to becoming the best version of myself again. I was also on my way to achieving that peace I desperately needed. Peace with myself, the people around me, and those circumstances that tortured me the most. Through months of therapy, I discovered that I lacked a sense of growth and consistency in my personal life, at home and in my relationships. Those are crucial to my need for meaning and fulfillment in this world. Again, if we're not changing, aka *evolving,* as individuals, wives, husbands, parents, lovers, and friends, what exactly are we doing day after day, year after year? During one therapy session, I was challenged to think about what it would look like to create boundaries between myself and the stressors that disrupt my peace of mind. This included people and situations that stunted my growth or contributed to the feelings of running in place. Boundaries that would allow me to have sustainable control over how certain triggers affected my well-being. What power did I have to create positive and sustainable change for my life?

The answer boiled down to another question my father would ask me when difficult circumstances overwhelmed me, "are you fed up?" In turn, I would reply with the obvious answer, "yes!" He'd say, "no, no, no...are you really fed up?" When a man or woman is fed up, they will go to extreme lengths to rid themselves of the anguish that plagues their mind, body, and spirit. It's the kind of anguish that cannot be prayed away. It requires action on the part of the host it infects. After all, as my father would say, "you ain't really fed up if it's still going on. When you really get fed up, you'll do what you gotta do." That was one of the best fatherly proverbs he ever shared with me. People will do whatever is necessary to be at peace with themselves and their life circumstances when they are genuinely fed up. I needed to create boundaries between myself, the people, and the circumstances contributing to the harm I was experiencing in my mind, body, and spirit. Boundaries that would get me back to being the best version of myself with resting peace. I was so fed up that losing income, being alienated from friends and family, or shaking up my marriage gave me zero pause. I was angry and beyond ready to go there. I was fed up!

My personal healing transformation began from the

inside and blossomed outwards. I had to critically examine what was happening inside of me, put a name to the areas that needed my attention most, and learn what was within my power to change for the better. My relationship with God was strong. I had the resources to help me restructure and reframe my circumstances. All that was left were the variables that would help to sustain the progress I'd made. A month after creating and testing a few boundaries, I knew I'd created sustainable change.

Boundary #1: *Pay attention to what is happening on the inside before giving your attention to the outside.*

I had to learn to listen to my body more intently. There were always warning indicators going off, but I snoozed and completely ignored them for all the wrong reasons. I was so consumed with any and everything outside of Alexis that I was unknowingly depleting myself of what I needed to be okay. There was no reserve and nothing set aside that was just for me.

Something special I didn't have to share. At one point, I'd made a mistake in thinking that maybe I wasn't meant to have anything special just for me. There was too much going on in my life to keep up with. How could I make significant room for Alexis without neglecting the needs of my children, marriage, or disrupting my relationship with other family members and friends? Some days I'd conclude that where I was in the grind of home and family life was the end of the road. I was convinced that I'd achieved all that life had to offer me until the kids were grown or until we made enough money to do more. The problem with that line of thinking is this: I belong to God before I belong to the cause of others. I am my own person before I am something for someone else. Maintaining a reserve just for Alexis gave me a sense of purpose beyond the service to my family and friends.

In marriage, couples should inspire one another to be the best version of themselves in every season they enter together. We are meant to consistently evolve as the seasons of life change. Who we were at 18 is not who we are meant to be at 25. Where the seasons of life take us at 35 should look radically different from our 25-year-old self. In our late 30s, married with children and a busy career, we should look forward to living our best life in our 40s. I can already sense a rebirth steering inside of me at 38, almost like I can burst into the next season of my life eagerly, ready to live it well. Life is far too precious to do less.

Inspire. It is a word that has driven me to continue to do what I do with a deep sense of purpose. I've always had the desire to not only be an inspiration to others but to inspire myself. After years of observation, experiences, and self-reflection, I've made some notable conclusions about how my life and relationship had to function for Alexis to be okay. I needed my spouse to encourage me to be the best version of myself, no matter how difficult the road of life would be. Not in an exhaustive, go, go, go type of way, but simply consistent. There's that word again. When we aren't the best version of ourselves, and there is constant friction with the people around us, we should question our contribution to the chaos. Put a name to the friction. Call it out, but don't be tempted to use permanent labels. It's easy to put permanent labels on yourself, people, and circumstances solely based on how things are in that particular season. My husband is a cheater and liar. My boss is racist and sexist. My in-law is psychotic. My wife is completely useless and lazy. My father is a deadbeat.

Labels are not helpful. Instead, call out what is causing the disconnect between you and the best version of yourself. Rather than laying out the shortcomings of others, it helps to examine our weak spots and the power we possess to create positive and sustainable change. Addiction, bad habits, dependency, poor choices, anger, a lack of patience, complacency, passivity, spinelessness, fear, narrowmindedness, selfishness, laziness...call it out. I allowed the day-to-day stress of work, home life, and relationships to compound and weigh me down. Point blank, I was holding onto stress, not communicating my frustrations, and I didn't say *no* enough. I treated my mind and body like a machine. Constantly producing, not really living. I allowed everything outside of myself to exhaust my time and energy. The stress was slowly chipping away at my body over time, and I didn't even realize how deeply it was affecting me until I broke. I'd grown accustomed to living with pain, never slowing down to even consider if it was something that could be eradicated. It was only a matter of time before I would experience the outward manifestation of what was breaking down internally. Boy, was there ever a need for boundaries. At that point, I needed life-saving boundaries.

Creating boundaries to take better care of myself came with considerable risks and rewards. There was a risk my family would not respond well to the need for distance from negativity and toxic drama. It's ironic how the people closest to you respond negatively when you tell them you're hurting and trying to eliminate unnecessary stress. Do not make the mistake of expecting support from the people closest to you. It's refreshing when/if it happens, but manage your expectations. Not everyone is on the same journey. It was totally within my control to create positive and sustainable change for myself, and I was ready to accept the risks associated with those changes. For me, it is counterproductive to carry the unnecessary weight of stress {pineapple!} while working towards a better version of myself. Prioritizing my mental and physical health was only the start of my journey.

Boundary #2: *Learn to love yourself before demanding the affection of others.*

Women like me sometimes sit around waiting for their husbands to surprise them with the same gestures of love year after year and baby after baby. During the first few years of our marriage, Brandon would wash my car, buy me the most beautiful and exotic flowers, get on one knee to ask me out on a date and surprise me at restaurants with gifts. Fast forward eight years, I would get so discouraged looking at empty flower vases after Hubby said he would always keep a rotation of fresh flowers. Those empty and dried out vases represented how I felt on the inside. Reminding and waiting on my husband to fill my love tank with the romantic gestures he used to lavish me with became a chore. Neither of us made our friendship and intimacy a priority. The spice and sparks in our relationship are what kept things fresh and motivated me to stay on my grind for my family. When our fourth baby girl was born, romance had officially left the building. Our marriage lost its flavor and the spark was non-existent. At that point, I began nagging Hubby out of frustration. The patience I once had to wait for the next romantic gesture turned into nagging reminders for him to remember to refill my love tank. Resentment kicked in when, as tired as I was with the work at home and the children, I kept his love tank regularly filled, always hoping it would be reciprocated just as intentionally. When it wasn't, I felt lonely and unworthy of affection. I knew my husband loved me and would do anything for me, but we found ourselves in a flameless rut. Work, children, extracurricular activities, and the routine at home was life. We stopped having fun.

154

Finding a babysitter on a Friday or Saturday night became impossible and expensive. Even if someone offered to babysit, I was too exhausted. Throwing on a pair of heels and walking out the door would have been a struggle for me. Being a wife and mother can be a thankless labor of love. Children work your nerves, husbands often don't know what to think when they come home, and mama is in a mood. Neglecting to communicate my frustrations wasn't helpful. It was all a confusing mess. After months of therapy, I had a revolutionary epiphany. Something in the nearly 40 years of living I had never thought of. It literally blew my mind, and I consider it a game-changer to this day. I thought to myself one day, *Alexis, have you ever bought yourself flowers? You used to love going to the movies during your single days. Why did you stop? Why are you nagging Brandon? Feed yourself!*

The truth was, I wasn't doing much of anything to create joy for myself. I'd unknowingly placed all the responsibility and pressure to make me happy on my husband. I was so utterly dependent on my man to fill

155

my love tank that I never stopped to consider what that pressure must be like from his perspective. Besides, nothing was preventing me from filling my own love tank. I just wanted it to come exclusively from Hubby. I was sitting in a sad pity pit, pressuring my man to give me the joy and happiness I needed to feel special as a woman, a wife, and now a stay-at-home mommy. My contribution to the lack of fun and excitement in my life and our marriage was equal to his, yet my frustrations were aimed solely at him alone. Getting back to what made Alexis smile and feel special, worthy, and appreciated meant I couldn't sit around waiting for anyone to fill my love tank or bring me joy. I had to take some responsibility for my own happiness. It was not my husband's sole responsibility in life to provide me with joy, happiness, and excitement. As lovely as that sounds, it is not realistic. Not to mention, it is way too much pressure to place on anyone. We were in the grinding years of child-rearing, the trenches. It's not fair to put unnecessary pressure on our loved ones. If the roles were reversed, I would feel extremely resentful if

156

every day I had to prioritize my spouse's happiness in life. That's a full-time job! It's not ideal, nor is it sustainable with all the children we have. Nothing was stopping me from getting to a place of fulfillment and contentment except... selfish and dependent Alexis.

There is nothing like looking forward to a vacation from the daily grind or setting time aside to get back to what you love to do. Lying on a beach for hours, listening to waves crashing against the shore while the sun kisses my skin, is all this mama needs to recharge. I prescribed myself annual mommy vacations. Once a year, I give myself permission to go anywhere I want for up to 14 days and do whatever makes my heart smile. It is my way to relax, rest, and recharge. No Hubby, no children. Naturally, Hubby was not fond of the idea at first. It wasn't the most exciting feeling in the world watching me pack a suitcase or dropping me off at the airport. He probably thought I would leave him with all the kids and never return! As radical as it may sound, it was a boundary line this mama had to create. It was my way to love and care for myself. Dedicating time to myself has been so rewarding for my physical, mental and spiritual health. I felt guilty the first time I packed for a trip to the Caribbean. I shamed myself for spending the money solely on myself, for daring to leave my children, and just dropping all my responsibilities at home to what... lay out on a beach for a week doing nothing? Yep! Again, creating and maintaining boundary lines can be difficult, and it looks different for each person. After my second annual mommy vacation, Hubby began encouraging me to get out more and have fun. He would buy me flowers and have them waiting for me in my hotel room. It didn't matter if I was in Jamaica, Costa Rica, or Spain. He made it a priority to send flowers ahead of me. Hubby noticed how incredibly refreshed and energized I'd be after returning from a mommy vacation and how generous I was towards his needs. Hello! Win-win!

Boundary #3: *Give yourself permission.*

Going from an arduous military lifestyle to being at home full-time was a huge transition. I did not give myself much time to transition into my new role at home. I should have thought more about what the tempo of homelife would be and what would work best in my new norm. Instead, I just jumped in headfirst. At the time, I thought, how hard could it be compared to the lifestyle that I was used to over my military tenure? My approach to transitioning from active duty to working at home full-time could have gone smoother. Even when I knew I was drowning and needed help, I made prideful and poor choices. I felt guilty at the thought of asking Hubby to do simple things around the house or with the children. Something as simple as asking him to change a diaper or clean the dishes made me hesitate. I didn't want to put what I perceived as unnecessary stress on him. He worked full-time outside of the home. I was at home all day with the children. I believed I couldn't ask much of him because he worked eight hours a day outside the home. I understood how daunting it could be to work all day and then come home to what felt like a second shift of more work. I figured he didn't ask me to go to the hospital with him to help clean surgical instruments, so asking for help juggling the work at home felt wrong.

Back in my single mother days, I stayed grindin'. I worked 10 to 12-hour days for the Navy, raised my son, took college classes, and hustled to climb leadership ladders at work. If I could do all that, it didn't seem reasonable to ask for help with anything I had 24 hours in a seven-day workweek to accomplish. Looking back, I could see how I was comparing apples to oranges. Within a few short years of being a full-time parent at home, I had never experienced more nervous breakdowns, anxiety attacks, migraines, stomach problems, backaches, and trouble falling asleep. Home life ran as smoothly as I could manage, but it came at a cost to my physical and mental well-being. If I exhibited any of these symptoms during my military days, I suppose I was too busy to give it much attention. The high-tempo military lifestyle did not afford much time to slow down and take notice of the physical and mental toll that it took on my body. It hit me like a bag of rocks. Working as a full-time stay-at-home mommy is no joke. I found out the hard way {pineapple!}. The days Hubby came home and knew I had a rough day, he would try to encourage me with words of affirmation. He'd tell me how beautiful I was, how grateful he was for a fresh start for our family, how blessed we were to have more time together, and how proud he was of my commitment to our home life. He would ask me at least three times a day verbally or through text messages, "have I told you how much I love you today and how proud I am of you?" Those words made my heart smile and reminded me of the bigger picture. We were doing a radically new thing for our family. Adjusting to the new norm would take time and patience. In the meantime, I needed something a little more than words. I needed tangible encouragement to get through my days, but I did not know how to ask.

Tangibly, I needed more from my teammate. At that time, Brandon and I were not functioning very well as teammates. It wasn't either of our faults. It was simply a lesson of what not to do. The day I recognized we were going about things booty butt backward, I knew we had to rethink how our partnership functioned moving forward. Even after acknowledging the problem and understanding what adjustments had to be made, I was very apprehensive about bringing it up to Hubby. I questioned why I was allowing the feelings of shame and guilt to disconnect me from the wonderful man I chose to do life with. It took physical exhaustion to remind myself that our family and home life were choices Hubby and I made together. It also made me wonder why my life partner was seemingly okay watching me juggle everything alone, rarely volunteering to pitch in and help out. It was a major contributing factor that led to my mental and physical break in 2020. However, my accountability in the chaos was that I wasn't expressing my frustrations to my husband. I had to learn to give myself permission to ask for what I needed. Like, *it's okay, Alexis, it's perfectly okay to ask your husband for help.* Imagine that. I had to learn to ask for what I needed as if it was built into my understanding that it was wrong to do otherwise. Draw your own conclusion about where I could have adopted such a stupid notion. The worst part was that I had a spouse who was more than willing to do what was necessary for our family. It amazes me how closed mouths can create such a ripple effect of chaos and confusion.

A year into my mental health treatment journey following the events of 2020, I asked my husband if he would be willing to take Apphia and Avigail to dance class on Tuesdays and Thursdays. This would allow me the time to get some much-needed work done around the house or if needed, quiet mommy time. It shouldn't have been a surprise to me when he happily obliged. When he got home from work, I asked if he would give me time to retreat to our bedroom for an hour so I could decompress from the busy day. Brandon was more than happy to read to the girls, arrange some daddy-daughter time outside, and do other helpful activities to give me that time. The problem was not that Hubby was okay with sitting around with his feet up while I was running around like Wonder Woman doing the most. He didn't think I needed the help and that he would mess things up, so he never bothered to get involved. He didn't notice how much of a toll home life had on me. I had to give myself permission to be vulnerable with my Hubby and stop making it seem like I had everything together. Things may have been running smoothly from the outside looking in, but it was pure madness trying to manage it all. I wasn't being selfish or lazy asking Hubby to hang up the clean clothes or take over the bath and bedtime routine with the girls. We have five children! Four of which are still small and living under our roof. There are six mouths and booties in our house. Raising a family is a full-time job with no paid overtime. Give yourself permission, mama.

Boundary #4: *Never stop dreaming.*

There was a time when I stopped dreaming. I was so bogged down with home and family life that there wasn't much space to dream (hmmm...is that a pun?). Pursuing personal goals most likely conflicts with the homeschool year or the children's extracurricular activities. Brandon's job was our family's sole source of income. His career and work schedule took priority. It wasn't a habit of mine to start something I couldn't see through to competition. In fact, it irritates me. Walking past a blank whiteboard in my bedroom was comically sadder. The way God wired me, I've always had an incessant desire to set goals and pursue dreams.

Hubby knows I would move mountains for him if he wanted to try a new career field or explore an idea. If we were tight on money, I could flip a dollar or create a financial plan to get him wherever he wanted in his dream quest. If my husband woke up each morning knowing he was on a path to being the best version of himself and living his purpose as a man, I would be more than happy for him. However, there was always a shift in enthusiasm when conversations surrounded my re-enrolling in school or starting the business I'd been dreaming of. The outcome of those conversations perturbed me over the years. Hubby was concerned about upsetting the stability of our home or, understandably, me getting burned out. On the occasions I brought up going back to school, the conversations would casually shift to Hubby talking about an issue at work or a potential opportunity to make a lateral career move. He'd then express the need for help brushing up his resume or navigating an application package. As annoying as it was, I'd oblige and wait for the next opportunity to revisit the conversation. After so many conversations being diverted, I gave up asking and dreaming altogether. Perhaps it was best if I waited until the children were teenagers or when they went off to college. Maybe it was best to save our family pennies for a couple more years before starting a business. Perhaps it would be best if Hubby and I focused on completing his career goals before beginning any new plans.

Not having a safe space to express a dream or explore a hopeful future is discouraging. I'm talking about dreams you lose sleep over {pineapple!}. Passions that wake you up at 3:00am to grab your tablet and write down the pathways and possibilities to success. With a drive like that, it's almost impossible to stay silent. I had to think critically about the factors within my control to create space to dream again and pursue personal goals. Once again, I had to remind myself I belonged to God before I belonged to the cause of others and that I was responsible for my happiness. Once again, I had to give myself permission. Permission to dream, explore, discover, pursue and accomplish. It didn't have to be a huge change, just progress. It could be one class a semester, one creative project a year, or $25/month towards a goal. Once again, I had to release myself from feelings of guilt or shame for making seemingly competing choices. Committing to family and home life is a labor of love and a noble cause, but I made a mistake; I stopped dreaming.

Support and encouragement look different for

everyone on the giving and receiving end. We don't all have the same drives and passions in life. After much discussion, Hubby and I learned that how we support one another is more complementary than equal. I've always been business savvy and driven, but the stress of such determination can weigh on my body and aggravate my nerves if it's not managed. Brandon knows how to balance me. He can calm me when I'm overwhelmed and distract me from the little things I allow to bother me too much. It's those blue eyes. They get me every time. Brandon is a romantic at heart, so he always has the words to make my heart smile. Because his primary love language is physical touch, I never have to ask for a back rub or a night of pampering while I talk his head off. We discovered that his style of support was precisely what I needed to dream again. All we had to do was put our heads together and put that partnership mindset to work.

Never stop dreaming. Evolving into the best version of yourself should be a continuous endeavor. Remember to reserve space for your dreams and passions, however big or small. There should always be room to be more intentional in broadening your perspectives, reframing your line of thinking, and applying what's discovered. If I get to a point in life where I'm so burnt out that I'm no longer dreaming or looking forward to a better future for my life, then it's time to create some healthy boundaries.

Conclusion

From the day I checked myself into the Veterans Affairs Medical Treatment Facility and through an 18-month health treatment plan, I can finally look at my reflection in the mirror and recognize myself. There wasn't a fractured or broken spirit desperately trying to make sense of life staring back at me. I'd established clear and sustainable boundaries that served as preventive medicine, keeping me from spiraling into dysfunctional behavioral and negative patterns of thought. Tested and healthy boundaries help prevent stress and the pressures of life from compounding and devouring me. The key is to never stop evolving. That means not allowing people or circumstances to stifle personal growth. I wake up with a clear purpose and am grateful for a more hopeful future. Even when my circumstances don't go how I'd want them to, I have considerably more control over how I allow them to affect me. I've never felt more empowered and capable. That power alone gives me a strong sense of security.

As I get older and learn more about myself, I remain open to reassessing my boundaries and adjusting those lines as needed to maintain my physical, mental and spiritual well-being. In the day-to-day, I have to remind myself to keep evolving. Change is a good thing, no matter how it makes me feel. My continued priority is to focus on my purpose and work toward what I'm most passionate about.

Here's the fine print. Creating boundaries does not mean neglecting responsibilities to marriage, family, and home life. It isn't a license to dishonor yourself, your marital vows, or your family. For me, boundaries were means of healing and rediscovery. They help protect my heart, mind, emotions, and spirit from forces in life that were eating away at me. Creating healthy boundaries and having those much-needed conversations with Hubby were some of the most difficult real talks we ever had. The struggle was 100% worth it! Setting boundaries helped me live intentionally in my season and reignited the fire and spice in our marriage. Prioritizing mental and physical health means saying *no*, a lot. Distancing yourself from toxic people and situations can feel like giving, as my daughters call it, the George finger. You know, from the movie *Rampage*? George loved to put up a specific finger at Dwayne Johnson's character. My girls would sometimes point with their George fingers to show me sometimes. I would say, "oh, no, sweetie, don't use your George finger. Next time, use your index finger to show me something." The point is, {pineapple!} it was challenging to create distance from people and situations that weren't conducive to positive and sustainable growth. It triggered feelings that were difficult to process and make sense of. My heart remains broken for the relationship I had to walk away from. On the other side of that process, I'm grateful to be delivered from chaos and dysfunction, both internally and externally. It's empowering to know I don't have to allow the projections of others to affect me. Narrow-minded perceptions of how married life should be or what a wife and mother can and can't do were laid to rest. My testimony in old age will not be of how I never fulfilled my dreams in life because something or someone held me back. Instead, my testimony will be written as AC Pearls in the books I leave for my children, grandchildren, and all who can benefit from its wisdom. There is freedom in reframing your circumstances and being intentional.

Time is your most precious commodity in this life, my sisters and brothers. I pray this book has encouraged and inspired you to make positive and sustainable changes for you and your family. Start fresh. Pray. Talk to God. Go slow. Heal. Be empowered. Do not allow people, fear, false perceptions, or toxic circumstances to stifle your growth. Be intentional. Be consistent. Embrace the journey, however difficult it may be. Above all else, love yourself.

www.ingramcontent.com/pod-product-compliance
Lightning Source LLC
Chambersburg PA
CBHW071438090426
42737CB00011B/1701